Letters to God

Letters to God
A Journey Through Infertility

Alissa Rieth

© 2008 by Alissa Rieth. All rights reserved.
2nd Printing 2014

Trusted Books is an imprint of Deep River Books. The views expressed or implied in this work are those of the author. To learn more about Deep River Books, go online to www.DeepRiverBooks.com.

No part of this publication may be reproduced, stored in a retrieval system, or transmitted in any way by any means—electronic, mechanical, photocopy, recording, or otherwise—without the prior permission of the copyright holder, except as provided by USA copyright law.

Unless otherwise noted, all Scriptures are taken from the *Holy Bible, New International Version*®, NIV®. Copyright © 1973, 1978, 1984 by the International Bible Society. Used by permission of Zondervan. All rights reserved.

Scripture references marked KJV are taken from the King James Version of the Bible.

Scripture references marked NASB are taken from the New American Standard Bible, © 1960, 1963, 1968, 1971, 1972, 1973, 1975, 1977 by The Lockman Foundation. Used by permission.

ISBN 13: 978-1-63269-037-1
Library of Congress Catalog Card Number: 2008903510

For Lee, Lucy, and our new little blessing, the three miracles of my life.

Acknowledgments

ABOVE ALL, I would like to thank my Heavenly Father for being my strength, my comfort, and my guide every day; for blessing my life abundantly; and for giving me the gracious gift of His Son. I would also like to thank all of my friends and family who prayed faithfully for Lee and me throughout this journey—your prayers were answered beautifully. Lee, thank you for loving me so generously and for being the soul mate I always dreamed of. Lucy, I thank you for filling my life with such joy and for greeting me each morning with that gorgeous smile. New little one, I can hardly wait to meet you. Mom and Dad, thank you for teaching me about Jesus, for showing me without a word how to make a marriage work, and for loving me unconditionally. Joshua, thank you for being the best little brother ever and for standing by me through it all. Darcy, thank you for looking at my manuscript with not only the eyes of an editor but also the eyes of a dear and treasured friend. I love you all very much.

Preface

MY HUSBAND, LEE, and I began this journey about five years ago. We had no idea what we were in for when we decided to start a family. We were full of excitement, anticipation, and hope for our future. We had been married for a little over two years, living in Ithaca, New York most of that time. Lee was working on his doctorate in chemistry, and I was working full-time as an engineer. It was September of 2000. Lee had just turned 31, and I was on the cusp of my 28th birthday. Our life was beautiful. We were in love and ready to create a new life from the love we shared. I had dreamed of being a mother ever since I was a little girl. I liked my job, but I knew that full-time motherhood was my true calling from God. I felt with every fiber of my being that God had created me to be a mother. A small part of me was anxious about the outcome, but I put that aside and instead flooded my mind with positive thoughts about our future family.

I have been a Christian for as long as I can remember. To me, it seems as if Jesus has always been present in my heart, filling me with peace and guiding my life. I have gone through times when I haven't relied on my faith and therefore have made some bad decisions, but looking back to those times, I can still see God's hand of protection on me. When we decided to start a family, I was at a point in my life where my job was taking up a good portion of my time and energy. I wasn't giving nearly enough time to God each day. I wasn't in the Word as much as I should have been, and my prayer time wasn't always productive because many times I would fall asleep halfway through. Needless to say, it wasn't the most fruitful time in my life, but I could feel a yearning in my heart to make time for God, to really quiet my life down enough to be still and listen for His voice.

After only four months of trying, we got pregnant. All my fears disappeared as I believed that I wasn't going to have any fertility problems; I was going to be fine. We were so excited and naively confident that all would go well. I started to dream about what our child would be like, and I started planning for our baby immediately. I made lists of all the things we would need, and we discussed names and read every book we could get our hands on about the miracle taking place in my body.

I remember with such clarity the day everything changed: I was about ten and a half weeks into my pregnancy. I started spotting in the afternoon, but I wasn't really worried. I had done enough reading to know that it isn't uncommon for a woman to have some spotting during her pregnancy, especially during the time when she would have gotten a period. I remember running errands with Lee that evening, starting to get bad cramps, and then the bleeding getting heavier. I knew then that something was wrong, but I still held out some hope that everything would be all right. I woke up in the middle of the night with cramps so painful that I couldn't stand up straight to walk to the bathroom. As I sat there with this life I already loved leaving my body, my husband sat with me, holding my hand, and we just wept.

An unexplainable sadness came and filled up that place where the life of my child once was, and I was so angry with God. I felt as if I had been tricked into believing that our dream was within reach, only to have it ripped out of our grasp. Somehow, though, in the midst of our pain, Lee and I became closer than ever before, even more sure that we belonged together. My anger at God eventually turned into a surrender of my control. I realized that He was the only one who could give me the strength and patience I needed to make it through this struggle. I pleaded for Him to lift me out of the fog of sadness I was living in and to help me somehow move forward with joy in my heart once again. He answered every prayer. I had come to God completely broken, wondering why things happened the way they did, and yet somehow I knew that

Preface

this was the only way I could really know Him and surrender myself to Him. I came to a point where I could say that I knew my miscarriage had happened for a reason. I didn't know what the reason was, but I trusted God enough to know that He had it all under control.

After three months, both Lee and I were physically, emotionally, and spiritually ready to start trying again. We had high hopes that we would get pregnant easily and things would work out. I didn't get a period the first month we tried, but every pregnancy test I took was negative. I still didn't get a period the next month, and all the pregnancy tests were, again, negative. I went to see my doctor, and he told me that I had a large ovarian cyst that was causing me to miss periods. We decided to wait for it to go away on its own rather than taking hormones to reduce it. The following month things were back to normal, and we were very ready to start trying.

At the end of September 2001, I had a very vivid dream that I still believe was a visit from God. Lee's mom, Lucy, had passed away in October of 2000, and we both missed her very much. Our baby would have been due right around her birthday (September 29th), and on that night, God comforted me in a way I didn't even know I needed. In my dream, I saw Lucy so clearly, dressed in a beautiful, glowing, white robe, holding a baby in her arms. She was looking down into the child's face and saying, "I will take care of little Emma." Emma was a name that we had talked about using for a girl. I woke up the next morning and remembered every detail of that dream so clearly. I told Lee about it, and we both felt that it was God's way of letting us know that our baby was with Him in heaven and that Lucy had a grandbaby to love and nurture there. It was so special and brought some closure to the grieving of our child.

As the months went by without getting pregnant, I felt my spirit begin slowly to fade. I couldn't understand what God was doing and why, but I wanted answers so badly. Meanwhile, almost everyone I knew was having no trouble at all starting a family. With each phone call about a new pregnancy or birth and with each shower invitation and birth announcement that came in the mail, I felt more and more inadequate and empty. It seemed like the natural and easy next step for all the couples we knew, but we were being left behind, while our friends marched on with their happy lives, making babies and becoming parents.

Then my brother, Joshua, called and told me that he and his wife, Ginny, were expecting. It took me completely by surprise. They hadn't even been married a year, and I had no idea that this was coming. I wanted so badly to be happy for them, and I tried to flood my mind with thoughts of how exciting it would be to have a little niece or nephew to love and dote on, but all that kept coming to my mind was, "Why them and not us?" It was this event, though, that finally brought me to my knees, crying aloud to God, abandoning any sense of myself, because I knew that it was only His love and strength that could get me through. I didn't know how to handle this news, and I honestly thought there was no way that I could make it through this trial in our lives. All that was left for me to do was beg God to give me the strength, courage, grace, and peace to rise above my feelings of complete hopelessness. Once again, He was right there to pick me up and carry me through this emotional struggle in my life. I started spending a lot more quality time with God after that, and He filled me up with all that I needed to keep marching forward each day, one step at a time.

By this time, we had been trying to conceive again for about eighteen months, and I had been through all the possible fertility tests that my regular OB/GYN could perform. Our next step was to see a fertility specialist. We decided to wait until we moved, since Lee was close to finishing his dissertation and was starting to look for jobs.

In February of 2003, we left our beloved Ithaca behind as we started another chapter in our life's journey together. We were headed to South Carolina and all the adventures it had in store for us. We bought our first house, and I started to believe that a family might not be too far off for us now. We had rooms to fill with little baby laughs and coos. Lee was starting his career as a chemist and I didn't have a job yet, so I thought for sure that the timing was perfect. But, again, months went by, and still nothing.

That spring we began to plan a garden for our new back yard, and we decided to dedicate it to Emma, the child we lost and still grieved. We had read somewhere that having a memorial for your miscarried child helped the grieving process. We worked hard to make it as beautiful as

Preface

we could that first year. It is and always will be a work in progress, but it will always be Emma's little garden.

Once we got moved in and settled, I started journaling my feelings on a more regular basis, as I had done so often when I was younger. It was therapeutic for me to get everything out on paper to God. It drew me closer to Him, and I found myself longing for my time with Him everyday. So the rest of my story unfolds from the pages of my journals, my letters to God…

Monday, April 21, 2003

LORD, YOU ARE so good! You have answered so many prayers in my life, in abundance. You have kept my family safe from harm, You have changed me for the better, You brought Lee into my life at a time when I thought I would never find my soul mate, You have blessed Lee and me with more than we need, and You have given me thirty years' worth of other answered prayers whispered to You in times of need and thankfulness. I know that You have a perfect plan for our family, but at times I get impatient and want to have my wishes fulfilled NOW! I long to have a child so badly. I long to look into its eyes and know that it is a child sent from You, a child created from the love Lee and I share. I still pray that one day I will know that feeling. For now, I have to pray for patience, to wait out Your plan; peace, knowing that You have everything taken care of; and faith, to come to You in my sadness and my joy.

Tuesday, April 22, 2003

I FEEL MORE AT peace today with our childlessness. Getting back into the Word has helped already. You are so much bigger than we are, with plans only to prosper us. I have to remember that when I start feeling sorry for myself. You truly have a beautiful plan for us!

Wednesday, April 23, 2003

TODAY HAS BEEN a great day of reflection and hope. I spent an hour (or two) at the Christian bookstore this morning, browsing through various literature, and finding some wonderful things to use for my devotion time. As I was driving home, I was speculating about various things I had read, and a thought came to me. Sometimes we have to ask ourselves, during trials and triumphs, if grace alone is enough to make us content. It should be, but is that how I am living my life? At first, I felt guilt for wanting a child, wanting stability, etc., but after thinking about it more, a peace came over me that I haven't felt in a while. Instead of worrying so much about what Your plan is for my life, I should concentrate on knowing that, even if I never have a child, I have the gift of Your grace, which is enough.

Thursday, April 24, 2003

I WENT TO A wonderful Bible study this morning. The lesson was on Abraham and Sarah (how appropriate). I felt like the leader was speaking right to me about truly waiting for the Lord. Abraham and Sarah were promised a son by You, God, but their impatience drove them to take the matter into their own hands. Abraham's son, Ishmael, who was conceived with his servant Hagar, was not Your promise; Isaac was. It was both comforting and confusing to hear that waiting is sometimes Your answer. Does this mean Lee and I should not pursue further treatment to get pregnant? Should we just be waiting on You, Lord? Father, I need guidance. I want to feel sure about what You are saying to me. I desperately want to do Your will, and I desperately want a child! How do I know what is from You and what I am deciding for myself? Help me to know and do Your will.

Friday, April 25, 2003

THANK YOU, FATHER, for my amazing, godly husband. Thank You for giving him such a generous and kind spirit. Last night we were talking about our priorities in life, and he said that his first priority was You, then our marriage/family, and then his work. As I think about our life together, I realize the truth in this. Lee gets up early in the morning to start his day by spending time with you, Lord. Then throughout his work day he calls me just to let me know that he is thinking of me, and he makes an effort to be home at a decent hour every night so that we can have dinner and spend time together. He lives out his life's priorities beautifully and with truth. He is a man of God, and I know that I don't show my appreciation as often as I should. I am so blessed to have him in my life. As I struggle to figure out what to do with my future, he is so supportive and just wants me to be happy. Please help me to encourage him in his faith walk, to strive to be a godly wife, and to be as kind and supportive to him as he has been to me. Thank You, thank You, thank You.

Wednesday, April 30, 2003

LORD, I AM feeling bad about a misunderstanding Lee and I had last night. It seems to happen at least once a month, usually right when we are supposed to be trying to conceive a child. Sometimes I wonder if Your hand is in it somehow. At times I think anxiety sets in because "we have to make love tonight." We have been having planned sex for two and a half years now, and I think it is wearing on both of us a little. We both long for a time when we can be intimate on our own time schedule and not nature's. Some months we can find the humor in it, and other months it's a struggle, but through all of this, I have learned some important skills. I have learned that praying for my husband rather than snapping at him is extremely healing for both of us. I have learned how to listen and communicate a little better. I have learned that sometimes taking a break from each other is just what we need to put things in perspective. And I have learned that in the end we both want the same thing, to love each other the best we can.

Thursday, May 1, 2003

FATHER, YOU ARE truly amazing! As I sat praying on my porch this afternoon, I felt so close to You. I thanked You for this gorgeous day and for allowing me the privilege of enjoying it. At the end of my prayer, I told You that I didn't understand why You hadn't made me a mother yet, and through tears I cried out to You for an answer. I wanted You to know that it was so hard for me to face each day wondering whether I would ever have a child and how I wished that I could just know the answer to that one question: Will it ever happen? I then turned to my devotion for the day in "Women of the Bible."[1] It was on Eve. The only piece of Scripture within the main devotion was "will give birth to children (Genesis 3:16)," and I heard Your voice speaking it to me. Talk about an instant answer to prayer! I felt so full of Your Spirit and at peace with my journey for the first time. I still have no idea what Your plan entails or what the exact timing is, but knowing that You have promised that we will have children someday is an amazing gift. Hearing Your voice today gives me hope beyond measure. Praise the Lord!!!

Friday, May 2, 2003

LORD, I HAVE been in a sad mood today, but I am not sure why. I should still be on a high from hearing You speak so clearly to me yesterday. Maybe it's because I believe that You have told me I will bear children, but I think my period is on the way. The first signs always make me a little sad. Help me to keep my thoughts focused on all the blessings in my life, especially Your grace and mercy.

Tuesday, May 6, 2003

I HAVE MANY THOUGHTS going through my head today. Lee just left for the airport—he is off to Houston for a conference, and I am feeling a little lonely. I sat down to read Your Word, and the loneliness has lessened. You fill so many needs, Lord. I am also feeling very confused, because I am having both pre-period symptoms and some early pregnancy symptoms. I know You can do anything, Father, so I want to believe that I could be pregnant, but I also don't want to get my hopes up and then be so sad and disappointed if I get my period. Please give me the strength to handle either outcome. You have told me that I will have a child, so now I wait…

Wednesday, May 7, 2003

I AM FEELING A little down again today. My period showed up this morning, which is always a big disappointment. It also means that I really need to decide about my future and forge ahead, but I don't see the path—I feel like I am in darkness. I know You will only reveal one step at a time, but I need to know what that step is. Reminders of Your promise have surrounded me today—a wonderful broadcast on the Christian radio station and my devotion on Sarah. I believe You will give me children, but I guess now is not the time. You have other plans for me right now. Light my path, Lord, and show me the way!

Thursday, May 8, 2003

I MISS LEE! I miss his big, gentle hand in mine and his sweet smile. I miss looking into his beautiful eyes and cuddling into "my spot." I miss his reassuring hugs and words that he so lovingly gives when I get my period. I pray that You will remind me of Your promise when I get sad, and also remind me that Your grace is enough. I am so blessed already in this life (Your Son, Lee, my family and friends, a roof over my head, financial stability—I could go on and on), and I'm not even truly home yet. I can't even fathom what that will be like—blessings beyond my imagination!

Friday, May 9, 2003

THANK YOU, LORD, for lifting my spirits. I feel better today—happier, content. Maybe it is because Lee will be back tonight, or maybe it was hearing the message on the radio this morning. It spoke right to me. It talked about waiting for You to reveal Your plan and doing it with a humble and believing heart. I am still waiting to know exactly how to proceed with my future, but I feel called to help others. At the end of the day, I want to know that I have helped make someone feel stronger and more confident about his or herself. Please help me to know how You want to use me. I don't want to follow any path but Yours. I believe Your promises, Father, and I long to do Your will.

Wednesday, May 14, 2003

LORD, SOMETIMES I am so confused as to why You put such a strong desire in my heart to be a mother but have not allowed us to conceive a child. I want so badly to raise children who love and honor You with their words and actions. I long to teach them of Your love and grace, and to learn even more about You with them. I must trust in Your promise that one day this will happen.

Thursday, May 15, 2003

I FEEL SO CLOSE to You right now, Lord. My devotion time has become one of my favorite parts of each day. I find myself longing to get into Your Word—to read more about You, learn more about Your ways, hear You speak to me, and see examples of how I need to improve my walk with You. I find my heart is less and less burdened with sadness over our infertility and more and more filled with hope to see how You will fulfill Your promise.

Monday, May 19, 2003

I AM FEELING A bit overwhelmed today, but I have come to realize that it is because of things that I, myself, have decided are important. Father, please help me during this week full of duties not to put aside my time with You for anything. I also talked to my brother this morning, and it sounds like their baby could come anytime. I was able to talk about it and not get upset. Thank You for answering my prayer for peace about their baby's upcoming arrival and for the ability to handle any talk of the baby with grace. It all comes from You…

Thursday, May 22, 2003

TODAY IS ONE of those cozy, rainy days that I enjoy every once in a while. I feel my pace slow, and my mind seems to have more time and space to ponder. I feel so warm inside as I sit to do my devotion with my cat cuddled up beside me. Thank You for days like this, Lord. I feel very at peace with things right now. I think being reassured of Your promises daily, as I read Your Word, helps. I pray that this peaceful feeling will last a good, long while.

Friday, May 30, 2003

I FIND MYSELF THINKING often about Josh and Ginny and their child that will arrive any day. I don't like the feelings of jealousy that rise up inside when I think of them getting a nursery ready, folding little baby clothes, or feeling their child move inside Ginny. I am working hard to fight those feelings, but it is very difficult sometimes. I also do have feelings of excitement and anticipation. This will be my first little niece or nephew—a new member of my family. Father, help me to fight this jealousy with love. Help me to accept that my time has not come yet and that this is meant to be.

Tuesday, June 3, 2003

I HAVE A NEW little nephew today! Tristan Evan has entered the world! I am actually doing pretty well with it and wishing I could meet him, hold him, and cuddle him. A little part of me wishes Lee and I were going through the miracle of having a child, but I have to believe in Your promise, God, that we will have children someday. My brother sounded so happy and content, which stirs my heart with so much emotion. Help me, Father, to shower this new life with honest love and to be **truly** happy for Josh and Ginny.

Thursday, June 5, 2003

(GENESIS 24)

SOMETIMES I WONDER if I haven't pleaded enough with You, God, for a child or prayed the right prayer. As I see how Eliezer prayed that God would show him who was to be Isaac's wife, it makes me wonder. He prayed so boldly and with such a specific request that he couldn't be ignored. But then I am reminded of Your beautifully clear promise, Lord, and my heart rests. I hear about people not really wanting children, but trying anyway "because all their friends are doing it," and it makes me angry. Please take this anger from me, and fill me up with joy and gladness.

Friday, June 6, 2003

HOW BLESSED I am to be celebrating five years of marriage to such an incredible man. Thank You today, Lord, for Lee and the beautiful marriage we have created. Even though I am sad that we don't have children, I know that Lee and I have used this time and our circumstances to become closer as a couple. We have grown in our faith and in our ability to communicate with each other. I think we will be better parents someday for having this valuable time together, just the two of us. I look with excitement toward all that You have in store for us in the future.

Wednesday, June 11, 2003

I REALLY WANT TO get into the habit of focusing on the blessings in my life rather than on the things I don't have. There are so few things that I NEED right now. I have all the material things I could ever need, and more. I want to focus on Your love for me, Your Son's sacrifice, and on letting others know what really matters, striving all the while to remember that grace is sufficient. I long for a child, and You have promised that I will bear children, so now I can focus my attention on building my faith and the faith of others.

Thursday, June 12, 2003

I HAD A REALIZATION while praying today, something I should have thought of a long time ago. Instead of complaining about the way others treat me or about their unsympathetic attitudes toward our situation, I need to pray, pray, pray. It is helping so much to be in Your Word everyday, Lord, but I still have days when things pierce my heart and bring tears to my eyes. I was at the pool yesterday, and all the other women there were mothers with their children. Innocently they ask if I have children, and when I say "no," the conversation ends because they don't know what to say or what else to talk about. Their lives are all wrapped up in their children, understandably, but that leaves me feeling alienated and reminded again of what I want so desperately.

Monday, June 16, 2003

I FEEL SO BLESSED right now. Lee and I had such a wonderful weekend together. I felt so close to him, and we just enjoyed each other. I am also feeling more content with our fertility issues. We have an appointment with a fertility specialist in two months. It is quite a wait, but I am relying on the fact that Your timing is perfect. We will have a baby when You are ready for us to have a baby, so the appointment is just a minor detail in the grand scheme of things. It's weird, but I feel like I know our child already, and I'm not even pregnant. Every time I look at Lee, I see a part of our child—I can't wait to meet him or her someday.

Wednesday, June 18, 2003

I AM STRUGGLING WITH my mixed feelings about calling my brother, and then I feel bad for feeling this way. I want to talk to him, but I know that there will be lots of talk about the baby, and I have to be in the right frame of mind to deal with that gracefully. One part of me totally understands how excited they are and that their world is consumed by this child, and I want to hear every detail so that I can get to know this new little person too. But another part of me feels hollow inside, aches for things to be different, and struggles with feelings of resentment and jealousy. Give me the courage and faith to listen to the part of me that celebrates with them and to be happy for the blessing of a new nephew to love and nurture.

Thursday, June 19, 2003

LORD, PLEASE HELP me not to get my hopes up too high this month about possibly being pregnant. My period is due in about six days, and I am once again trying to predict what is going to happen based on every single thing my body does. "What does that little cramp mean?" "Oh, I woke up in the middle of the night to go to the bathroom, maybe I'm pregnant!" "My breasts aren't tender yet, maybe I'm pregnant." "I'm feeling bloated, I must not be pregnant again this month"—and so on and so on. I make myself crazy, but as hard as I try, I can't stop myself from thinking these things each month. I guess all I can do is ask that You will diminish the disappointment if I find out it didn't happen again. Fill my heart with praises either way.

Thursday, June 26, 2003

THAT SAD FEELING is growing this morning. I don't have my period yet, but I am pretty sure that it will appear imminently. I have to try to focus on the positive—that we have an appointment in a month and a half with a specialist so we can try to figure out what may be wrong. I just want a child so badly that I hold out hope until the last possible moment, and then I am disappointed again. You commanded all Your people to procreate and we can't. It makes me feel like a failure—like I am being punished. Am I?

Friday, June 27, 2003

THERE HAVE BEEN lots of tears and much heartache today. I got my period last night, and needless to say, I was devastated. Today has been a hard day. I thought I had prepared my heart for another disappointment. But when it actually happens, and there is no longer any possible way that this miracle might have taken place, the tears come and the knowledge that at least another month of waiting is in order overwhelms me. Each time I go through all the emotions—anger, sadness, disappointment, frustration, hurt, despair, longing, and more. I don't know which one is the right one to feel, so I just go numb after a while. Help me make it through the next few days and beyond until I hold my child in my arms.

Tuesday, July 1, 2003

A FEELING OF CONTENTEDNESS is with me today. I feel so wrapped up in Your love, Lord. You have blessed me beyond measure, and I want to thank and praise You over and over. Your Son paying the price for my sins is all that is needed in this life, and it still amazes me that, because of that gift of grace, You see me as blameless, sinless, white as snow. And yet I have been blessed in such abundance beyond that. I have the most wonderful, godly husband, a loving family, and the luxury to sit here and ponder Your Word everyday. "Thank You" doesn't even begin to measure up to the praise You deserve.

Wednesday, July 2, 2003

LORD, YOUR TIMING and Your plan are baffling to me. As I look back on my life, I see times when I thought You weren't with me or when I thought something **should** happen because I just knew the timing was perfect. When it finally did happen, I realized that You were always there with me and that Your timing was truly perfect. Help me to keep that in mind now as I wait for Your timing concerning a family for Lee and me. You have given me a promise that I believe in, so it is no longer a question of if, but when. Help me also to be patient and trust in Your plan.

Thursday, July 10, 2003
(Romans 14 and 15)

*H*OW HUMBLING YOUR words can be, Lord. And we need to hear them, maybe today more than ever. Romans 14 and 15 spoke to me today and pointed out how glaringly judgmental and harsh I can be at times. I need Your help to work on extending a genuinely kind and caring hand to everyone—fellow Christians and non-Christians. We all have our views that extend beyond the laws You have given us, and in the end, they don't matter. Help me to embrace those that have different views than I do. Help me to see them as Your creations and to be a light and example to them of Your love.

Wednesday, July 16, 2003

I HAVE BEEN THINKING about what I need to work on as a Christian wife. I find myself at times not being as supportive as I should. I know that I can be too judgmental and crabby with Lee for no reason. I just ask that You help me to work on my attitude toward Lee. Give me a calm presence and an encouraging manner when he tells me about things at work. Allow me to be as supportive of his other relationships as he is of mine. I truly want him to be able to establish meaningful male friendships, so please help me to encourage anything that will foster that. Help me to be a godly wife.

Thursday, July 17, 2003

I CAN FEEL THE two possibilities rearing their heads in my mind. I need strength, Father, to keep them at bay until I know the answer for sure this month. Then I will need Your help to deal with all the feelings that will arise with either outcome. I feel myself getting excited again at the possibility that this is "the month," but I also feel dread arising as I think about dealing with another month of disappointment. Keep my eyes on You, Lord, so that Your promise will be on my tongue and either outcome will leave me knowing that Your will is done.

Tuesday, July 22, 2003
(Matthew 6)

*L*ORD, I NEED patience today! I can feel my excitement building over the possibility of being pregnant. It is already two days past when I normally get my period, and there is absolutely NO sign of it yet. However, I should know by now that it can happen so fast—nothing, and then cramps ten minutes later. It is constantly on my mind today, and I am having trouble concentrating on my responsibilities. Help me to keep my focus and to realize that thinking or worrying about it will do no good. Thank You for my very appropriate reading today. Do not worry…

Thursday, July 24, 2003

I COME TO YOU today, Lord, with a broken heart and an aching soul. Another month of not being pregnant, and I can feel it starting to wear me down. I have been in tears on and off since yesterday afternoon, and I have been afraid to talk with You because of my anger. I am also very worried now about how this will affect me when I see Josh, Ginny, and Tristan in a few days. I just wish I could have You physically walking beside me, with Your hand in mine, all this next week. I have good intentions about my attitude, but I know that I will have to be really strong to hold to those intentions. The problem is that I am not feeling very strong at all right now. I feel inadequate, jealous, sad, pitiful—all ugly and unchristlike things. They have this beautiful, new baby boy, and our arms are still empty. How do I fight these jealous feelings? How do I get over the thought that they have been smiled down upon by You while we have been passed by? I know that isn't true, but my human heart still lets the thought enter my mind. I can only do this with Your help and strength. Be near me, Father.

Friday, July 25, 2003

I AM FEELING A little better about things today. I am not so weepy and sad, although I am still a little worried about how everything will go this week at the lake during our family vacation in Minnesota. It will be the first time that I have seen Josh and Ginny with Tristan. I feel that I have prepared myself as best I can, and I have spent a lot of time in prayer about it. I have prayed that I will have an attitude of love, that my emotions won't get the best of me, and for Your strength to get me through every situation. The shield of prayer is always at my disposal, and I have asked that You will remind me to call on You when things get difficult. Thank You for that gift and for loving me through my anger.

Monday, August 4, 2003

WHAT A RELAXING week! It was so wonderful to be surrounded by family and to enjoy the beauty of Minnesota. Thank You, Father, for giving me the strength and grace to keep my emotions in check all week. It was so amazing to meet my new little nephew. He is so beautiful, and I can't wait to get to know him as he grows. Those feelings drowned out any thoughts of jealousy or emptiness. You make all things good—PRAISE GOD!!!!!!

Friday, August 8, 2003

I HAVE BEEN THINKING a lot today about our upcoming appointment with the fertility specialist on Monday. I am excited and anxious to start trying something new, but I am also scared. Once we get to the end of this journey, we will have a child or we won't—only You know. If we don't, that means we will have tried everything we can to have a child of our own. What happens if we get to that point? I could make myself crazy thinking about this possibility. I have to remember that there are still many things that we can try and that You have a perfect plan for our future. Be with us through this journey we are about to embark on, Lord.

Monday, August 11, 2003

I HAVE FELT YOU near and have felt Your hand of blessing upon Lee and me these last few days. We visited a new church on Sunday and really enjoyed it, but it is about 40 minutes from home, which we don't think is very practical. However, we met a man there who was so nice and really made us feel at home. When we arrived at our appointment this morning, the doctor came in to meet us, and it was the same man from the church. I felt instantly comfortable with him, knowing he was a Christian, and his kindness reassured us both. He suggested we move forward by trying an IUI (intrauterine insemination) next cycle. I am scared but also very excited.

Thursday, August 14, 2003

TODAY IS MY beloved Lee's birthday. Thank You, Lord, for creating him exactly as he is. He is my soul mate, my prince charming, the love of my life, and the one I dreamed of but thought I would never find. You brought him to me at exactly the right time, and my love continues to grow for him daily. He is so kind, generous, sweet, handsome, strong, capable, sympathetic, funny, trustworthy, responsible, faithful, God-fearing…and he's MY husband. What a blessing You have bestowed upon me. To have been loved by him in this life is one of the most beautiful gifts You have given me.

Monday, August 18, 2003

MY CYCLE OFFICIALLY began this weekend, which means we are starting the IUI process. I am really excited to try something new, but along with that excitement is a little apprehension. Now that there are new possibilities, we have more reason to believe it could work and, therefore, farther to fall if it doesn't. I am telling myself that I will be okay if this first one doesn't work, but the further along we get in this process, the more the options start to diminish. Help me to keep my spirits up and my hopes high, and to be reassured by Your promise.

Tuesday, August 19, 2003

SOMETIMES YOUR WORD confuses me, Father. I read today in Matthew 21 that "if You believe, You will receive whatever You ask for in prayer." I believe in You, Lord. I believe You sent Your Son to wash away my sin. I believe that because of Your Son's sacrifice I will spend eternal life in Your presence. And I have earnestly asked and prayed for a child that Lee and I can raise to love and serve You. Is there something harmful in that request? Is it just that it's not Your will to give us a child right now? I don't understand, but I will keep searching and praying.

Wednesday, August 20, 2003

I AM FEELING A bit overwhelmed right now, trying to follow all the instructions for IUI and getting organized for the two weekend trips we have coming up. I am going to take today to regroup a little, plan the rest of my week, and make sure I understand everything for this IUI process. I just pray that You will help me to keep my eyes on You, Lord. I can accomplish anything with You by my side. I will need strength, comfort, and guidance in the days ahead. And I will need reminders of Your beautiful promise.

Thursday, August 21, 2003

I HAD A NICE, long talk with a dear friend on the phone today—it was so refreshing and renewing. Lord, You have given me so many beloved, Christian friends. They are all beautiful women, inside and out, who can make me laugh, reassure me, guide me, and cheer me on in my faith and my everyday life. Help me to nurture and strengthen all my friendships, Father, with Christians and non-Christians. Help me be a light of Your love to those who don't know You and a help in strengthening the faith of those who do know You as their Creator and King.

Friday, August 22, 2003

MY DEVOTION TODAY told me to write a letter to You, Father. Since I write to You everyday about my worries and concerns, I want today's letter to be all about You! Thank You for this beautiful day and for calling me Your Beloved. You are an awesome God, holy and mighty. You are always there waiting, with Your hand extended, if I would just reach out. I long to grow even closer to You, to realize every day what a gift Your grace is, and to have that be enough for me. I want to love You with wild abandon, as You so deserve.

Tuesday, August 26, 2003

MY TIME IN prayer today was so refreshing. I felt so near to You, Father, and so calm in Your presence. I feel like I am learning to truly lay my worries at Your throne and rest in You. You know what the next few months will hold for me, and that is such a great comfort to me. Why worry when You have it all figured out? Help me to remember this on days when I don't feel at peace or as near to You as I do today.

Thursday, August 28, 2003

I AM STARTING TO get really excited about the possibility of being pregnant this month. All of my tests have gone really well so far. Today they did an ultrasound of my uterus and ovaries. My follicles are plump and ready to release eggs, and the lining of my uterus is perfect—a lush environment for an egg to thrive. Now I just have to wait for my hormones to peak, and off we go to have the procedure done. They will do a pregnancy test two weeks later if I haven't gotten my period. I know I will be excited, so please, Lord, give me the strength to deal with either outcome.

Monday, September 1, 2003

WE HAD OUR IUI done on Saturday. I am excited to think that there may be a life growing inside of me right now. I want to keep the right perspective on this though. I must continue praying that Your will be done, and if that means this is not the right time for a child, help me to accept that. Draw me close to You, Father, so that Your will is truly what I desire in my life. You have inscribed me on Your hand, and You only want what is best for me. Why is that so hard for me to remember in the midst of the struggles?

Tuesday, September 9, 2003

*M*Y ANXIETY IS growing as the day for a pregnancy test draws near. I am waiting for my period to come and yet looking for any sign that I could be pregnant also. For some reason, I feel confident that I am pregnant, but I have felt this way before and been wrong. I need Your guidance, Father, as Lee and I navigate this possibly stormy season. If I am pregnant, I will be worried about miscarrying again, and if I am not, I will, of course, be disappointed and worried that it won't ever work. Then I worry about all the moral issues ahead of us if IUI doesn't work. Keep me patient and calm.

Thursday, September 11, 2003

HOW APPROPRIATE THAT I would have such a lousy day today, September 11th. I got my period, cried in front of everyone at small group, and found out our doctor wants to jump right to IVF (invitro fertilization) next. I don't even know what to do right now. I am heartbroken, angry, sad, scared, and overwhelmed. There are so many moral issues connected with IVF—things I didn't think I would have to face so soon. What are we supposed to do, Lord? I am pleading for You to guide us.

Friday, September 12, 2003

I READ THROUGH PSALM 139 various times yesterday and today for Bible study. How amazing You are, Lord. To be reminded that You know everything about me is such a comfort. You knew what part I would play in this world before I was even born or conceived. You see that I will fail many times over, and yet Your love remains constant and strong. I feel so lost right now and long to know what path to follow—which path is yours? Guide me, Father.

Monday, September 15, 2003

FATHER, I FEEL so confused and lost right now. I have such a strong desire to be a mother, but You have not allowed that to happen yet. Our only remaining option is to try IVF, which I am just not sure about. I feel like I am trying to make decisions that only You can make: how many eggs to implant, how many babies we want at one time. Is it right to move ahead, Lord? Is this Your will or is my desire driving this decision? Help me to make sense of it all.

Tuesday, September 16, 2003

(Ephesians 1:3–14)

As I read this scripture today, something jumped out at me. In both verses 5 and 9, the word "pleasant" is used to describe how You feel about adopting us according to Your will. How wonderful to know that it pleases You to have me as Your child. How comforting to know that You have a perfect plan for my life and that it gives You pleasure when I walk in that will. How amazing to know that there is probably a smile on Your face when I follow through and do Your will. It makes me want to please You even more.

Wednesday, September 17, 2003

LAST NIGHT LEE and I went to a seminar on infertility, and it helped me to understand and feel better about our options. It was reassuring to see what they base their decisions on for IVF. I feel confident in their ability to guide us through this. Yesterday, when reading 1 Corinthians 10, I ran across a section talking about not getting caught up in the legalistic things of this world. The notes in my Bible said that we have freedom to do things not specifically mentioned in Scripture. I thought maybe that was telling me IVF is okay and not to worry. Then I thought about the fact that the notes are written by man, not You. It is something to ponder…

Friday, September 26, 2003
(Psalm 104)

How beautiful this psalm is. I am always amazed when I open Your Word to find what beauty, majesty, and comfort lay within its pages. There was a time when I didn't understand the power of the Psalms, but You have shown me over and over the beauty in them. The beginning and end of this psalm are perfect bookends, praising You mightily. The rest of the psalm so wonderfully describes Your power. It makes me ponder again why it is that I worry about things, since You have control and You love me and will watch over me.

Wednesday, October 1, 2003

(Psalm 104)

AS I READ this psalm again, it just cements for me the fact that it is all in Your control. You have put everything on this earth, and You can take it away. You created the earth, the sun, the stars—everything to work with such perfection. The sun rises and sets every day because of Your perfect work. You are always pleased with Your work, because it is made by You, the one, true, perfect God. But what about us? We disappoint You every day, and yet Your love continues. How do You see us? Because of Jesus, perfect, I guess. This thought brings me to my knees in humility.

Friday, October 3, 2003

TODAY I JUST want to write every detail of Your beautiful visit to me, Lord. I was in my yoga/Pilates class on Wednesday morning, and at the end of class, during the meditation/prayer time, I saw a vision of You. I was walking through the most beautiful garden I had ever seen, and there were angels singing (probably because the music playing at this time sounds like what I think the voices of angels sound like). I saw a bright light ahead of me, and I started walking toward it. As I got closer, I saw You with Your arms stretched out, inviting me in. You had a dark, olive complexion; shoulder-length, dark hair; and the kindest, most loving eyes I have ever gazed into. I ran to You, and Your arms enveloped me in such a warm, comforting, and tender embrace that I didn't want it to end. Then You placed Your hands on each side of my face and lifted it up so I could look into Your beautiful eyes. Tears welled up in both of our eyes, and You said to me, "Dear, sweet child, I know You are hurting, but Your faith in me will get You through. Everything is going to be all right." You then wiped the tears from my face and smiled at me. Our visit ended there, but it will live in my heart for a long time. Thank You for this precious gift, Lord. I know that at times when I am sad or discouraged I can remember this vision and again feel Your tender embrace and Your soft hands wiping my tears away. It is a reminder to me that You hurt along with me, and yet You also know that the hardships are necessary to build my character and faith. I feel closer to You right now than I ever have in my life. My heart feels truly peaceful, and it makes me long for Your return. I find myself hoping that our baby Emma can look into Your eyes every day in heaven and know that she is blessed.

Monday, October 6, 2003

(COLOSSIANS 3:1–17)

I LOVE THIS PASSAGE of Scripture. It will always hold a dear place in my heart because a portion of it was read at our wedding. I feel like it so completely tells us how we should treat each other and how to live a life pleasing to You. As I read verse 3, where it says that "our lives are hidden in Christ," it made me think about how we are such imperfect creatures and how only through Your Son's sacrifice are we washed white as snow, perfect in Your eyes. This passage is a good reminder of how to treat everyone in my life: forgive, love, and grow together. What beautiful instructions!

Tuesday, October 7, 2003

(Genesis 2)

How amazing life is! The first man was created from dust and Your breath, God, and then we all descended from him. I wonder what Adam was like; I wonder how it felt to be in such close proximity to You and to be perfect. The whole concept of how a life is created baffles me sometimes. As we have struggled to create a life, it amazes me that this complex process actually works for couples as often as it does. As I ponder whether or not there is a new life inside me right now after waiting so long, I am blown away by the possibilities, happy and sad, that may lie ahead.

Wednesday, October 8, 2003

I AM SO CONFUSED, Lord. My period is now three days late, but I did a pregnancy test last night and it was negative. I want to believe that we just did the test too early, but that is unlikely. Maybe I have another cyst, or maybe my period is just going to be really late this month. But why? If I'm not pregnant, why must I endure this torture? All I know to do is ask for Your strength and patience, once again, to get through this.

Friday, October 10, 2003

I AM FEELING DISCOURAGED about things right now. I know You would never deliberately hurt me, Lord, but this last cycle I felt played with. I found myself getting so excited and thinking that You were fulfilling Your promise, but then I was proven wrong at the last minute. Why, Lord? It is difficult enough to have to deal with not being able to conceive, but to have late periods and other signs that trick me into thinking my time has finally come is torturous.

Monday, October 13, 2003

WE ARE GETTING ready to go back to see our fertility specialist today. I am still feeling so confused, like I am wandering around not knowing where to turn. I don't know what to do about IVF—is it what we are supposed to do, or by doing it, am I being a Sarah? I know You have promised me that I will give birth to children, but is doing IVF taking things into my own hands as Sarah did by using Hagar to have a child? This child would still be a part of both Lee and me, just with a little extra help. Where do we go from here? Do You think I would not be a good mother right now? I need Your guidance.

Tuesday, October 14, 2003

(EPHESIANS 5:21–33)

AM I THIS wife? Do I submit to Lee in everything? Does he love me as his own body? This is definitely something that needs to be read in the midst of our struggles together. How beautiful that marriage between a man and a woman is compared to Christ's relationship with us. I love the parallels drawn with baptism and redemption. Lee and I must remember that we are one flesh now, a team, with You as our leader and Christ as our coach. We need to feel and care for each other as we do our own bodies, always nurturing and loving!

Wednesday, October 15, 2003

(Ephesians 5:21–33)

AS I PONDER this passage further, it really makes me think about how I treat Lee and others in my life. Do I treat my marriage to Lee with the same respect that I treat my relationship to You? Not as much as I should. You compare marriage to Your relationship with us, and I need to start looking at my marriage with the same eyes. Even in my relationships with other people I should be treating them more like You treat me, Father. I guess that is what we should all be striving for in this life—to be more like Christ. Help me to shower those around me, especially my husband, with Christ-like love.

Monday, October 20, 2003

(ROMANS 5:12–20)

THIS IS AN awesome comparison of Adam and Christ. Alike physically, but each brought totally different things to the world—Adam brought condemnation/sin, and Christ brought righteousness. Christ's gift takes Adam's legacy of sin away. This makes me realize again how great a gift salvation is, how miraculous. I don't deserve such a thing, and yet, it's mine for free. That should be enough for me in this life, but sometimes I let my desires interfere with that—a child, beauty, possessions. Remind me daily of Your grace, Lord!

Tuesday, October 28, 2003

(Genesis 3)

AS I READ Genesis 3, I saw You asking Adam and Eve questions that You already knew the answers to, Lord. I think You did that to make them speak their wrongdoing. The wrong becomes so much more real when You have to tell someone out loud what You have done. It also put the disobedience on them, since they had to admit to it. If You still actually spoke out loud to people today, what question would You ask me? What am I trying to hide from You that You see plainly in my heart? What is it I would have to own up to?

Tuesday, November 4, 2003

(EPHESIANS 1:3–14)

THE IDEA THAT You knew everything about me before You even created this world is so amazing. You wanted me to be holy and blameless, but because of sin, I am not. Your beautiful plan takes care of that, though. The gift of Your Son washes away all the sinfulness that is in me so that I am presented to You as flawless, without a blemish. How do I begin to thank You for Your gift of grace? What words measure up to the greatness of Your sacrifice? And yet we can still bring You pleasure! I don't think I will ever be able to fathom how big Your love is while I am in this world. To look You in the eye when I get to heaven will be the most humbling and beautiful moment. This life—every moment, every sadness, every accomplishment—is part of the plan You orchestrated. I make my choices (and many have not been what You wanted for me), but You make even the bad choices fit into Your plan for my life. Do You ever get tired of my complaining, my anger that things aren't going my way? I apologize and place myself in Your hands. Guide me, Lord.

Tuesday, November 10, 2003

(Genesis 6)

OH, TO HAVE faith like Noah. He didn't even bat an eyelash when You asked him to do this monumental and strange task. You have given me promises, Lord, but I still find myself doubting them or trying to bargain with You to have things my way rather than yours. Noah didn't ask any questions or second-guess Your instructions. Help me to learn to put my complete trust in You, even when this world gets me down. You are faithful to all Your promises, and You know the best way—I just need reminding.

Monday, November 17, 2003
(Genesis 8)

I NEED A DOSE of Noah's patience, Lord. He was so calm in Your plan. How do I do that? Some days I feel so strong—that I can wait patiently for Your plan to take shape—and other days, like today, I feel so defeated. Why is it that Lee and I seem to have so many obstacles in our path? How much more can I handle? I need Your hand upon me right now, Father. Remind me of Your amazing love and grace that should be enough. Stop all the negative thoughts about age and timing. Give me peace and comfort to keep moving forward along the path You have for me.

Friday, November 21, 2003

FATHER, I DON'T even know exactly how to begin writing today. There is so much whirling around in my head and my heart. I can't deny Your clear promise that I will give birth to children, and I have been praying earnestly for You to block our way if IVF is the wrong choice for us. Now I feel that I am at a crossroads, and I need Your guidance and strength even more. Is this odd, early cycle I am dealing with right now the roadblock, or is it just Your way of getting the timing right? In my purely human brain it still isn't clear, but I truly want to do Your will. Please make each step clear to both Lee and me so that we can walk in Your way.

Thursday, December 4, 2003

(Genesis 11:1–9)

THIS STORY OF the tower of Babel brings to mind all the towers that I try to build for human reasons and not to glorify You, Lord. I want to have the right attitude toward You and not be so worried about having the right clothes, having the prettiest house, etc. I know that these things don't really matter, but I let myself get caught up in it. My eyes are no longer on You but on the things of this world. Lord, help me to keep my perspective and, when I start to get caught up in worldly passions, find peace in knowing that I have eternal life with You.

Friday, December 5, 2003

(LUKE 3 & ACTS 2:1–13)

WHEN I READ this story of Pentecost I always wonder what it would have been like to be there. What exactly did the tongues of fire look like? What did it feel like to be in the midst of this miracle? I still see Your miracles, Lord, and I am so thankful that You have shown yourself to me so clearly and beautifully. When I was reading Luke 3 today, I read a footnote about how Your son waited patiently in Nazareth until he was 30 years old to begin his ministry. Help me to follow that example, to be reminded daily of Your perfect plan for my life. Praise be to God!

Wednesday, January 7, 2004

(Hebrews 11:8–10)

LORD, I SOMETIMES complain about going new places or doing things I haven't done before, because, I am afraid of the unknown. Abraham followed Your commands without second-guessing or questioning Your reasons. He was a much better person than I am. Did he ever doubt? Did he ever cry out for answers as he waited for Your promises to be fulfilled? I feel so guilty for my impatience in waiting for Your promise of a child. I want to scream out, "When???" Three and a half years is minor in comparison to Abraham's wait. Give me patience!

Thursday, January 8, 2004

LORD, I JUST have to get down on paper Your blessings for me today and the wonderful feeling of Your constant presence. I prayed with all my heart yesterday that I would feel Your strength and presence to get me through what I thought would be a hard day. Not only did You answer that prayer but also many more along the way. This was supposed to be our last month to try IUI, and the fertility medication didn't seem to be working. I wasn't getting any high ovulation readings on my fertility monitor as the days of my cycle passed by. I tested again yesterday, right before my doctor's appointment, and my first prayer was answered—a peak reading! I continued to feel You with me throughout the day as I prepared for my IUI this morning. It was almost as if I could feel Your hand in mine, and it was such a comfort. Then, as I was driving to the doctor's office this morning, the sky was filled with the most amazing pink and purple colors from the sunrise. The sun was shining through the huge, rippled clouds. As I was looking at the sky I saw for a split second hundreds of beautiful angels in the clouds guiding my way. I got goose bumps all over, and tears filled my eyes. You showed me beyond a doubt that You were with me, and no matter what happens You will always be with me. I have seen and felt Your hand in everything over the last few months, and I want to believe it may mean this is it, this time it is going to work. My heart is guarded, though, because of all the times I have been wrong in the past. Please forgive me for being timid about where this is leading. No matter what the outcome, I know that You have answered prayer after prayer and blessed me with Your strength and presence. You have shown me what to do each step of the way. I want to shout my praises to everyone, "You are the Almighty One, my Comforter, Best Friend, Healer, and Counselor. Hallelujah!" I truly believe that each one of those angels in the sky today was there because of a prayer sent up for me by someone that loves me here on earth. So, thank You for all the dear friends and family that pray so earnestly for us. What more can I say but I love You, Father, and thank You, thank You, thank You.

Monday, January 12, 2004

(Philippians 3:12–4:1)

IT IS COMFORTING to read that we should forget our past. So often I think that my hard times now are somehow punishment for my past. Maybe it is a consequence of my sin, but I think that You are more worried about my journey forward, my attitude today. How difficult it is to follow what Paul said—to press on and keep my eyes on You no matter what my past looks like or what worldly things are going on around me. This is definitely something to strive for daily.

Tuesday, January 13, 2004

(PHILIPPIANS 3:12–4:1)

IT IS SO interesting to think about the fact that during Paul's time Christians had to rely on the example of Paul, and others like him, because they didn't have the Bible as a guide. I know Paul wasn't perfect (he even says so himself in this passage), but he must have been an exceptional Christian man if You chose him to be an example to all those he preached to. I think about what I would be like in the same position. Could I live up to what Paul accomplished? Would I be a good example to all those I was in contact with? Even though we have Your Word as a guide now, we still need to strive to shine the light of hope and love to everyone. Thank You, Lord, for giving us Your Word. Help me in each situation to act as if I am the only source others will have to know Your love.

Friday, January 16, 2004

LORD, I AM trying to be patient and keep my eyes focused on You, but it is difficult. This first week of waiting for the results of this IUI went pretty fast, but this next week is going to be very hard. I am just waiting for any signs of my period or of pregnancy. I know in my head that no matter what happens it is part of Your plan, but I find my heart hoping this is it. I try to rationalize every little thing I am feeling—every cramp, discomfort, or pain. Help me to remain patient and ready for any outcome.

Wednesday, January 21, 2004

I AM HAVING A hard time concentrating on my devotion today. My mind is elsewhere, and my heart is heavy. I don't know for sure that I am not pregnant, but I started spotting today, so I am pretty sure that my period is on the way. I am trying not to get too upset about it yet, but at the same time, I am trying to wrap my arms around another disappointment. I am trying to understand what all of this means, if anything. All I know to do right now is pray for peace.

Friday, January 23, 2004

LORD, I WANT to thank and praise You a thousand times over for the peace You have given me in answer to my prayers. Since this IUI didn't work, the one thing left to try is IVF, and I was so anxious yesterday about whether or not moving forward was right. I still have no idea what Your ultimate plan is for Lee and me as parents, but I know it will be beautiful. I have prayed so boldly for You to stop us if IVF isn't right, and instead, I feel like obstacles have been removed. Your being so near to me during our IUI makes me believe that I am in Your will, even though it didn't work. I wouldn't have made it through this journey without You, Father.

Monday, January 26, 2004
(Genesis 15)

I KNOW ABRAM WASN'T perfect, but what an example he is to me of true faith. So many times when You told him what You were going to do he listened and accepted it with incredible faith and trust. I am beginning to see how You are using my journey to strengthen my faith, Father. As Lee and I began our lives together in Ithaca, You were right there beside us. I can see clearly how You touched both of our lives with people and circumstances that have influenced our decisions and our faith. My life is so much fuller and richer because of the time we spent there, the friendships we made, and the life we started. We began to dream about our future family there, and from the first prayer I uttered, asking You to bless my womb, I have felt You guiding me. Each step along the way has made me stronger, built my character, and brought me closer to You.

Wednesday, January 28, 2004

LORD, I WAS talking to a friend today, and she mentioned something that really struck me. I have been praying that You will put an obstacle in our way if we are not to do IVF, but I don't believe You have done that yet. However, if IVF isn't going to work because You want us to adopt before we have children of our own, please reveal that to me. I have to learn not to base all my decisions on feelings, so I need to know for certain whether we should or shouldn't move forward right now. I truly want to do Your will, and I pray that You will keep me walking in it.

Thursday, January 29, 2004
(Romans 1:18–31)

LORD, SOMETIMES I wish I had all the right words to say to unbelievers and those who question Your existence. I feel like this passage in Romans is so important and could be shared with those who aren't sure about their faith. Every single human being has a knowledge of You in his or her heart, and each has chosen to embrace it fully, fight it continually, or outwardly acts as if he or she accepts it but then fails to follow through. In our hearts it is so much easier to accept You than to fight You, but the outside world makes it seem like it is so much easier and more exciting to reject You. Enable me to live out my love for You daily, shining Your light like a star for the world to see.

Monday, February 2, 2004

*L*ORD, I AM amazed daily by how You work in my life. Over the last few years I have grown so much in my faith. Because of that, I can see You more clearly at work around me. Even six months ago I don't know if I could have prayed for You to put an obstacle in the path of IVF if it wasn't Your will. Now that I am bold enough to pray it, I feel more at the center of Your will than ever before. I truly want to follow the path You have for me. Give me the strength and ability to see the next step. Thank You, my Shepherd, for leading this lost sheep.

Wednesday, February 4, 2004

I HAVE TO ADMIT that sometimes I don't understand Your plan, Lord. I found out yesterday that another person I know is pregnant. I am having a little harder time with this one, because it is someone who was only trying because all her friends were trying. Why them and not us? I struggle so often to understand why some people are blessed with children they don't want, can't take care of, or have just to keep up in their social circles, and yet those blessings pass us by. Lee and I long to be parents. We yearn to take on the responsibility of caring for another human life and of teaching our child all about Your love. This is one of the many questions I want to ask You when I finally see You someday. Help me, this side of heaven, to wait patiently for my turn, and fill my heart with peace.

Tuesday, February 24, 2004

WHY DO I so easily forget Your promise to me? I was crushed today when I got the news that I have a cyst on my ovary, which means we have to postpone IVF a week. I was so sad and angry but, as always, reading the Word today helped put things in perspective. I am very confident that I am walking in Your will for me, so this must be from You somehow. It may be a timing thing or something else that I can't foresee, but You can and You are watching out for me. Help me to remember that.

Wednesday, February 25, 2004

I HAVE SO MANY thoughts and feelings whirling around in my head and heart today. I saw the movie "The Passion of Christ" last night, and it was so moving. It made me see Jesus' sacrifice in a whole new way. Jesus came so willingly to save us who sin daily. I can't even fathom that love! The movie was so hard to watch at times, but how could I cover my eyes when I did those things to Your Son too? I wanted to yell out loud at the Roman soldiers to stop whipping Jesus, but how could I when I sin multiple times every day? Each of our sins is like another crack of the whip on Your Son's back, and yet we sin with such ease. I can't stop thinking about my part in it all.

Monday, March 1, 2004

FATHER, I REALIZE more and more each day what a gift You have given to Lee and me as we await the fulfillment of Your promise. It is only through You that we have had patience, strength, peace, and perseverance to make it along this journey. There is nothing left in me that gets me through; it is only You. Maybe that's one of the things You wanted me to realize in all this. I still don't know how long we will have to wait, but to know we are on the path You marked out for us before we were born continues to give me hope.

Tuesday, March 2, 2004

(Isaiah 53)

THIS PASSAGE IS another poignant reminder of what You did for me. Jesus was so brave to leave heaven to come to earth, and You let Him go. Wow! You did all this for us, poor, miserable sinners. Who am I to question Your timing and Your plan? I found out today that our IVF has to be postponed another week because I still have the cyst on my ovary. At first I started to pray for the cyst to go away, but then I realized that might not be the right thing to do. This could all be part of Your divine timing. All I can pray for is that Your will be done and for patience to wait that out.

Friday, March 5, 2004

(Genesis 16)

THIS CHAPTER IN Genesis really hits home for me in my current situation. I see Sarai and Abram taking things into their own hands to fulfill Your promise to them. But all it produced was Ishmael, not Isaac who was the promised son. Again I ask, are Lee and I doing this same thing with IVF? I have prayed so much about this, asking You to reveal to us if we are on the wrong path, but instead I believe that You are showing us that we are in Your will and to trust You. I feel so strongly that this cyst is a part of Your timing and that I shouldn't choose to do anything to make it go away. You will allow that to happen on its own. Please continue to reveal Your plan step by step, Lord.

Saturday, March 6, 2004

I FEEL LIKE I am in someone else's body now that I am on fertility drugs. So far it hasn't been as bad as I had heard it would be, but it is strange. Sometimes something so trivial will upset me, and I know that I shouldn't be getting so angry over something so insignificant, but I can't make my emotions fall in line. I just cry and think the world will never be the same. It feels so silly to write this, but it is exactly what happens and how I feel at the time. I sure hope this is all worth it. Lord, help me to control my emotions and turn my concerns over to You.

Monday, March 8, 2004

(1 KINGS 19:1–18)

LORD, HAVE I missed Your gentle whispers? I know that I have heard many of them, but I wonder how many I have missed because I have been too busy, too stressed, or too tired to really listen. Why does Elijah repeat his lament again after he hears Your whisper? What did Your whisper say? It doesn't seem like he changed at all after hearing You. I can see myself in this as I look back over my journal entries for the last few months. I have asked You the same question so often, even when I think I have heard Your answer. Give me the conviction to believe and stop questioning.

Friday, March 12, 2004

AS PART OF my devotion today, Father, I looked up various verses that contained the many names we have for You. The most meaningful names to me have always been Shepherd and Comforter, but the one that specifically spoke to me today was Father of Compassion (2 Corinthians 1:3). You know my hurts, my trials, and my struggles, and because Jesus came to earth, He truly knows how I feel and has compassion. Thank You for sending Your Son to earth and Your Holy Spirit into my heart. I know that without You I would be lost in this crazy world.

Monday, March 15, 2004

(Genesis 18)

I HAVE LEARNED SO much in the last year from Sarah. I ask myself often if I am making the same mistakes she made, and at times I want to laugh at Your promise to me too. I can hardly imagine anymore what it would be like to be a mother. But Sarah's story has also been a good reminder to me that You will always fulfill Your promises. I want a child so badly, but I can honestly say now that I want Your will for my life more.

Wednesday, March 17, 2004

(John 17)

THIS CHAPTER OF John seems so personal to me for two reasons. First, it is Jesus' personal prayer to You before He died. It feels like I am sitting at His feet while He prays. Second, He prays for us all, including me personally. How touching to hear Jesus praying for me. Sometimes it blows my mind that You know me and love me so personally. What a gift! I know the love You have for me, Father, is immeasurable. Thank You.

Tuesday, March 23, 2004

(LUKE 17:26–36)

IT IS REASSURING to hear that You are coming for me, Lord. I know so confidently that I have eternal life in You, so the second coming doesn't scare me at all. However, as Luke writes about not going back for things in Your house, I think about what I would do in that situation. I worry that I won't know that it is You or that I will worry about my family first rather than running to be with You. Please give me the wisdom and discernment to know it's You and to have my eyes fixed so firmly on You that this world will have no ties to me.

Wednesday, March 24, 2004

AS MY IVF transfer day approaches tomorrow, I am feeling a little nervous about the decisions that may need to be made about our embryos. I pray that they are all viable enough to be implanted or frozen so that there aren't any hard decisions to be made. Father, all I can do is ask for Your guidance, wisdom, and discernment if these issues arise. I want so much to be in Your will, so I pray that the next step will be revealed clearly. I want so much for this to work, but I also know that You know what is best.

Friday, March 26, 2004

OH, GOD, YOU are so good! As I sit here looking at the picture of our two embryos, I am truly amazed. You are the Creator of life, and the fact that I may be carrying life within me now overwhelms me. I have seen You so much this week: in Elizabeth being the woman in my devotion, through the nurse at the hospital today who proudly proclaimed Your goodness, by giving us sweet friends that have faithfully prayed, and by taking care of our embryos so that we didn't have to make any hard decisions. You are so present in my life, and I truly believe that I am walking in Your ways no matter what happens. I hope the time has come for You to fulfill Your promise!

Tuesday, March 30, 2004

(Genesis 22:1–19; Deuteronomy 8:1–5)

How Your Word speaks to me, Father!—the testing of Abraham and the words in Deuteronomy, "just as a man disciplines his son, so the Lord Your God disciplines You." I think I have always known that this waiting was a test, but now it seems clear. You humbled me by taking my ability to conceive away, which has caused me to truly hunger for You. Now I must believe that You will send the manna (children) as You promised. I definitely would not have been the same mother three years ago as I would be today. I have so much more to offer now, and I want to continue to learn so that I can become an even better mother.

Wednesday, March 31, 2004

ANXIOUSNESS IS SETTING in as I wait to find out next week whether or not I am pregnant. I truly want Your will to be done, Lord, but I am scared that Your will is that I am not pregnant. I know it will be really difficult for me if the test is negative, but I also have to know that You wouldn't do that if I couldn't handle it. I am worried for Lee also. He is a little down right now, and more bad news is not what he needs. I ask that You watch over him, and help him to realize that his worries are of this world but that he belongs to You. Allow me to be encouraging, supportive, and caring as I minister to his needs.

Monday, April 5, 2004

I AM SO RESTLESS today, Father, as I wait for my big test tomorrow. I have no reason to believe that this hasn't worked, but there is definitely a part of me that is holding back because of the possibility of overwhelming heartache. Only You know the full outcome, Lord, and I know that Your will is what is best for us, but sometimes I feel like I can't take another disappointment. I have learned so much and grown in my faith by leaps and bounds on this journey, but only You know if I am truly ready to be a mother.

Tuesday, April 6, 2004

TODAY IS A big day. I am sitting on my porch in the warm sunshine awaiting the results of my pregnancy test. My heart is very anxious, so I have been trying to calm myself down with prayer and Your Word. Has the time come, Lord? Or must we continue to be patient and wait for Your promise to be fulfilled? I believe so strongly that the path we are on is the right one—why have us do IVF if it isn't going to work? I am worried about how Lee and I will deal with a negative result. Right now I feel as if it may cripple us emotionally. I beg You to be with both of us, Father.

PRAISE GOD! The phone rang as I finished writing earlier, and it was the doctor's office—I am pregnant! I don't even know where to begin to thank You for this blessing. We have waited so long and have only made it through because of the strength and patience You gave us. Now I pray that You will bless my womb and keep this child safe until I hold him or her in my arms. I know this child is a gift from You, Lord, a special child that You created to come to us at exactly the right time. What else can I say but thank You for this blessing.

Wednesday, April 7, 2004

(Exodus 25:1–9; John 14)

IT IS BAFFLING to me how specific You are with Moses here. Why these specific things? I do find comfort in the fact that You wanted the tabernacle built so that You could dwell among the Israelites. Today You dwell inside each of Your believers through the Holy Spirit. How wonderful to have You inside our hearts. As I read John 14 today, I was reminded of this same thing, and I also realized that I must give this worry about my pregnancy to You. If I know I am in Your will and You will do what is best for me, why worry? I must trust and believe.

Tuesday, April 13, 2004

*I*HAD MORE GOOD news from the doctor today. My hormone levels are continuing to go up normally, which means I am still sustaining a pregnancy. I am feeling good about all this. I feel so wrapped up in Your will and in the prayers of so many people. I pray, Father, that You will continue to protect this new life inside me. Help me prepare to take on this honorable responsibility of motherhood. I believe that my most important task will be to teach this child about You, Your son, and Your amazing love and forgiveness. I know I have so much more to learn, but I feel very ready for the task that lies ahead of me.

Tuesday, April 20, 2004
(John 14:1–7)

OH, WHAT A thought—that You are preparing a perfect place for us and that You will come for us when it is ready. I can't even fathom what it will be like, how beautiful, how perfect. We will be able to again see those we have been missing. I don't deserve such a place, but You love me anyway and gladly continue to prepare it. Did this miracle child growing inside me come from that place? I feel like it did—a true gift from You, given only after I humbled myself and obeyed. I feel like I will see a bit of You in this child's eyes.

Wednesday, April 21, 2004
(Hebrews 9:23–28)

ONE ACT WIPED us clean—how beautiful and how unworthy we are. I love to see the parallels between what You had the people do as rituals before Christ came and Christ's death and resurrection itself. How I want to be able to teach these things to my children. I want them to see Jesus in every Bible story and in every person they meet. I want them to long for a personal relationship with You. I guess all I can do is start praying now and never stop. I can teach them what I know and live as I would want my children to live. The rest is in Your hands.

Friday, April 30, 2004

FATHER, SOMETIMES I am so overwhelmed by the promise You have fulfilled with this beautiful life inside me. It still doesn't feel real to me that I am finally going to be a mother. My journey has been a struggle, but I have grown so much. I feel so much closer to You and more confident of my faith. The biggest lesson I have learned is to trust completely that Your will is the best way. The fact that I was able to pray for You to put an obstacle in our way if we weren't supposed to do IVF, and then truly to know in my heart that I would not do it if that happened, was a big step for me. I know there were times when I doubted Your promise to me, but deep in my heart I knew You would follow through in Your time. Through this I have heard Your voice, become more faithful, and witnessed the power of prayer. Thank You for blessing me so abundantly, for drawing me closer to You, for disciplining me in Your ways, and for loving me unconditionally. I love You, Lord.

Tuesday, May 11, 2004

AS MY CHILD grows inside me, I realize how much I want him or her to know about You, Father. I pray that You will continue to mold me so that I can lead my child to You through example. Guide me in my decisions and actions so that what my child sees me do will be the right thing. I know that I will falter at times, so I pray that You give me a humble heart to apologize and forgive easily. Be with me always.

Monday, May 17, 2004

I AM REALLY STARTING to get more excited about my pregnancy now that we have hit the ten-week mark. Father, I just pray that You continue to keep this life safe within me. Since my last miscarriage happened at ten and a half weeks, I will feel so much better if we can get through this next week. I want to write a journal to my unborn child, but I am afraid to start yet, knowing how heart-wrenching it would be to have begun if something does happen. Please continue to give me peace and strength. Help me to stop worrying and instead to concentrate on keeping myself healthy so this baby will be strong.

Tuesday, May 18, 2004

(Genesis 12:1–5; Acts 7:2–5; Hebrews 11:8–10)

ABRAHAM WAS SO faithful! How do I get there? How do I reach that point where I don't question Your voice any longer? I know that I am closer than I ever have been, but I still don't think I have the faith Abraham had. I realize that he wasn't perfect, but he was so strong, and he put all his trust in You. I pray that You continue to mold me, Lord, so that I can become the person You want me to be. Help me to let go of my silly, worldly concerns and focus instead on nurturing my relationship with You. This world will pass away, but You will be with me always.

Thursday, May 20, 2004

I WAS SO WORRIED yesterday when I started spotting slightly. I think part of it was that I am at exactly the same point I was when I miscarried before. My prayers were answered though, because today everything seems fine. I am still feeling unattractive as my body begins to change, but I have to forget about that and concentrate on keeping this baby healthy. God, You made me exactly how I am, and I must love myself right where I am at. You are preparing my body for a miracle—I should be happy about that after waiting so long.

Monday, May 24, 2004

FATHER, I WRITE today with a heavy heart and so many questions. I have lost another child, watched motherhood slip through my fingers once again, and I can't even begin to understand. Why were we given hope if it would be torn from us? My arms feel so empty, and I never actually held this child, but I loved him with all my heart already. I say "him" because I had drawn so many parallels between our story and Abraham and Sarah's story that I thought of this child as a little Isaac. Am I being punished? What lesson am I to learn now? Dear, sweet friends of ours gave us a dogwood tree to plant in memorial. Lee and I planted our little "Isaac" tree on Saturday. The act of planting it together helped some, and it is therapeutic to have a reminder of this child. Now we have Emma's garden and Isaac's tree—our world is full of memorials rather than children we can hold and love. What good will come of this horrible pain? I wish You could give me that answer right now; somehow it seems like that would fill an empty space inside me. As most all of my friends prepare for motherhood or immerse themselves in it, I have to wonder why I must wait. Do You think Lee and I wouldn't be good parents? Are You trying to tell us to stop? Or must we forge ahead and pray that someday the pain will lessen and we will have our arms filled?

Tuesday, May 25, 2004

(Deuteronomy 1)

AS I READ this first chapter of Deuteronomy this morning, I was able to parallel certain aspects of the Israelite's journey with my own faith walk. Instead of trusting in You, they grumbled and complained, thinking You had led them out of Egypt only to hand them over to the Amorites. All along You had planned only what was best for them, but they didn't obey You or trust You. They brought suffering upon themselves by their own selfish desires and sinful nature. I do the same thing so often—I allow myself to think that I know better than You do what is best for me. I don't obey or trust You as I should. I find myself thinking my plan makes more sense than Yours does. Why do I allow myself to do this almost every day, Father? As I continue to struggle with the emotions of my miscarriage, I am amazed at what Your Word can do—it is so healing. I pray that You will continue to speak to me.

Thursday, May 27, 2004

IN YOU, FATHER, I have found peace. I can't even begin to understand how I would be getting through this without You. It is only by the strength, patience, and peace that You have bestowed on me that I am able to keep going each day. I don't know why I am on this particular journey, but I am certain that I am exactly where You want me to be, and I find some contentment in that. I am already seeing good coming from my trials as in my pain I minister to a friend. I ask that You continue to give me the words to bring her closer to You...

Tuesday, June 1, 2004

(PHILIPPIANS 4:11–13)

AS I BEGIN this new Bible study, "Calm My Anxious Heart,"[2] with some of my close girlfriends, I find myself looking forward to the truths You will reveal to me throughout these twelve weeks. One of the first things it asks us to do is define contentment. This is somewhat daunting to me since I am not really feeling content right now. My heart still aches for our lost child, and I often wish things were different. I wish I was still pregnant, looking forward to becoming a mother. Instead, I feel empty and sad when I think about the possibility of Lee and me never having children of our own. I have dreamed about having children with Lee practically since the first time I met him. Sometimes when I look at him I feel like I get little glimpses of what our children might look like. Will there ever be a child in this world that is part of the two of us? Thoughts like this consume me daily. I am hoping that this study will allow me to get my focus back on You and the relationship we have.

I suppose I would define contentment as relying on You for my strength and being full of joy in any circumstance. If I truly let You be the Blessed Controller of my circumstances, I would feel so at peace. I could really accept that each step I take was marked out for me before I was born. During hard times, I could completely rest in the knowledge that You are working out the best plan for my life. Help me to let go, a little each day, of the things I am trying to control. Help me give them up to You.

Wednesday, June 2, 2004

(Philippians 4:11–13)

LORD, YOU HAVE all power, You are sovereign, and You long to take over all the worries of my life. You can give me all the strength I need for each day. I must give up control and begin learning how to be truly content. I must focus on today, realize how blessed I am, stop complaining, and leave tomorrow to You. Whatever may come is from You, and You will only give me what I can handle. Each hardship brings me ever closer to You, makes me more trusting of Your plan and more willing to let go and fix my eyes on You.

Thursday, June 3, 2004
(Philippians 4:11–13)

Heavenly Father, thank You for willingly taking the role of Controller of my life. Help me to focus on what is truly important and to learn contentment no matter what my circumstances. Allow me to feel Your presence so that letting go will be easier. Take the spiritual gifts You have given me and show me how to use them to glorify You. Burn Your words into my heart so that I can call on them at all times.

Tuesday, June 8, 2004

(Philippians 4:6–8)

AS I MAKE lists of the positives and negatives in my life for Bible study, it is very clear to me that the positives far outweigh the negatives. I need to learn to start counting my blessings more often, especially when the negatives start to creep into my thinking. The negative thing I tend to dwell on most of all, obviously, is the fact that I am not a mother. It is easy to let it pervade my thoughts, since most of the people I interact with everyday are either pregnant or have children. I have a choice to stop being anxious about it, though. I should present my worries to You in prayer and then let them go and allow Your peace to fill me up. In the past, when I have felt Your peace wash over me and You took the weight of all my worries away, it brought me such a sense of calm. It seems to leave me too quickly, though, because I let it be crowded out by everyday concerns, and eventually, I am weighed down again and call out for Your help. I want to learn to carry that peace with me always so that it crowds out the worries. You have the best life planned for me, so why do I worry each step of the way? As I pray, Father, help me to remember to start with my thanksgivings. It is usually harder to complain once I have thought of all the beauty in my life.

Wednesday, June 9, 2004
(Philippians 4:6–8)

I HAVE WAITED SO long to be a mother, and as I continue to wait, I find that I am learning skills that I will need—patience, perseverance, trust in Your ultimate plan, and contentedness. I surprised myself when one of the first things I said to Lee after we lost a second child was, "Thank God we have each other." I did not have that same mindset or response after our first miscarriage. Looking back, I can see how far I have come, and I can only imagine how far I have yet to go. Why do I forget that Your Word is the best instruction guide for life? I have always known it, but I don't always remember it when I need it most. What more could I ask than to have someone willingly take my load of anxieties from me? It seems that the more I wish I didn't have to worry about something the harder I cling to it. You want to take the burden from me, and I keep holding on for dear life. Why is that? All I should be doing is keeping my mind focused on true, noble, right, pure, lovely, admirable, excellent, and praiseworthy things. I need to loosen my grip on the negative so that the positive can flow through me and fill me with Your grace.

Friday, June 11, 2004

(Philippians 4:6–8)

THANK YOU, FATHER, for blessing my life with so much love and beauty. Help me to recall all these things when life's worries start to burden me. Allow me to ask You to take these anxieties and burdens from me so that I can focus on things You have instructed me to think about. If nothing else, bring to mind the greatest blessing of all, the gift of Your Son. Let me let go and open my heart to Your perfect plan for my life.

Tuesday, June 15, 2004
(Matthew 20:28)

THIS WEEK IN my study, we are talking about being content with the various roles You have given us in our lives. I find myself concentrating so much on myself lately rather than others. I am so consumed with dealing with all my emotions that I have forgotten that I am here to serve. I really need to stop spending time having a little "pity party" for myself and instead reach out to help others in their need. Father, give me the grace to follow through on this, to stop grumbling about the petty things happening in my life, and to start looking out rather than in.

Thursday, June 17, 2004
(Psalm 139)

I OFTEN FIND MYSELF wishing I could be a mother when I see other women with their children. I find it especially hard when I see a woman with children the ages my children would now be had they remained here with me. As I read over Psalm 139, I realize again that You don't want me to do this. You knew each of those children I had in my womb, and they are now with You rather than with me. Only You know when my time to be a mother will come, and it will be in Your perfect timing.

Friday, June 18, 2004

(Matthew 20:28)

AS I THINK about the roles You have given me, I realize that above all I must be faithful in them. I must constantly remind myself what You expect of me in each role and then honestly seek to fulfill the responsibilities given to me. I also must treasure each role, honor each role, and never belittle or degrade myself in the process. Only You, Lord, know when each role will begin and end, and I must find contentment in that. My role as a mother will start exactly when it is supposed to, and I must be quiet and wait for You to tell me what role to tackle in the meantime.

Monday, June 21, 2004

I AM SUPPOSED TO write a letter to Lee as part of my study this week, telling him what I love and appreciate about him. Give me the words, Father...

My Dearest Lee,

I don't know where to begin to tell you everything I love and appreciate about you. Most importantly, I appreciate the relationship you have with God. I love watching your large, manly hands as they turn the fragile pages of your Bible and how you so honestly seek His truths. As we pray together at night, I love to hear your deep voice call out to God with thanksgiving and the pain-filled voice that honestly seeks Him in times of trial.

I love that your support of me is constant and holds only one condition—that I am happy. Your generous and kind spirit moves me almost daily as you reach out to those in need or offer up your help to any person or group that You believe honestly needs it.

I love your sensitive, loving side that feeds my need for affection and romance. I love that you cry easily but still command such a strong, manly presence. I love that you can cry with me and still wipe my tears away and make me feel so protected.

I love your sense of humor and spontaneity. I love that we laugh a lot and truly enjoy each other's company. You can turn my bad moods into good with just a glimpse of that gorgeous smile of yours. I am the most blessed woman on earth to be able to call you my own.

Friday, June 25, 2004

I HAVE BEEN THINKING a lot today about my future. What do You have in store for me, Father? When will I ever be a mother? Is there more pain ahead before Your promise is finally fulfilled? I get so frustrated as I wonder why You picked this journey for me to be on. My yearning to be a mother only gets stronger each day rather than dying away, even with each painful step I take. I worry about my age and whether I am doing the right thing. Please take these worries and anxieties from me, Lord, and replace them with comforting thoughts of Your love and sovereignty.

Monday, June 28, 2004

YOU ARE SO good, God! You answered my prayer by filling my thoughts this weekend with reminders of Your almighty power and amazing love. I kept remembering something we had read a couple weeks ago for Bible study, and I have gone back to reread it many times in the last few days. I think writing it out will help it to really sink into my thoughts so that I can recall it whenever I need it.

- Never allow yourself to complain about anything—not even the weather.
- Never picture yourself in any other circumstances or someplace else.
- Never compare your lot with another's.
- Never allow yourself to wish this or that had been otherwise.
- Never dwell on tomorrow—remember that [tomorrow] is God's, not ours.[3]

Help me to think this way all the time. Allow my paths to be straight and to lead straight to You.

Tuesday, July 6, 2004

FATHER, YOU KNOW how my heart aches for a child, and You know each worry in my heart. Therefore, You are well aware of my anxiety over my age. I feel that as I get older my body is less and less likely to become pregnant, and I wonder whether it will ever happen. I dwell on all these things instead of giving them up to You and letting them go. I may have to pray for You to take them from me every day, but I know that I must do it. Help me to let go.

Monday, July 12, 2004
(1 Peter 5:6–7)

*T*HESE VERSES REALLY affected me as I meditated on them today. I must hand over all control to You, Father, so that I may humble myself under Your mighty hand. I must not assert my own power over You, because You are the ultimate authority. I have to do this with a genuine attitude of submission, or it will never truly work. I have to remember daily that You have my best interest at heart, and all You do or allow to happen in my life is done out of pure love. There is good to come of all trials—lessons to be learned and things to be better understood. You can see my entire future, so why not hand it all over to the Great Omniscient One? You have instructed me to cast all my anxieties on You. You want to take them from me—what a gift. Keep my eyes on You, Lord, and remind me that Your shoulders are ready to take on my worries.

Thursday, July 15, 2004
(Matthew 6:25–34)

*Y*OU TOLD YOUR disciples so clearly not to worry, Lord. How wonderful to have Your words in Matthew to read every day. We don't listen any better though. We let our worries run our lives. We let them get in the way of loving and praising You. We find comfort in them somehow. Calm my anxious heart and the thoughts that grow into worries. Remind me that You will always get me through any difficulty. I must live in the current moment and leave the worries of this world to You.

Monday, July 19, 2004

(Hebrews 11:1)

WHAT IS FAITH? I think this verse is a perfect definition. Faith is being certain that, whatever happens in my life, even in the lowest, darkest moments, You have a perfect plan at work. It is trusting that You will get me through the hard times, molding my character along the way to become more like Christ. Keep my faith from ever faltering, Father, and allow it to continue to blossom more each day.

Wednesday, July 21, 2004

TODAY I ASK that You reveal more of Your character to me. I long to know every detail of who You are and how You work. As I wait for children, I should be spending my time learning as much about You as I can so that I can teach them all I know. I want to live each day by faith rather than by my own fickle human feelings. Guide me through this difficult time, knowing that You are always faithful.

Monday, July 26, 2004

YOU HAVE BROUGHT me so far emotionally over the last couple months, Lord. I was so anxious in May after I miscarried a second time. My body had less energy, and it was a struggle to get motivated to do much. My mind was working overtime, thinking about how I was only getting older, worrying that something was wrong with me physically. My spirit was empty, wondering "why me?" and I was angry with You. I was judging You, God, by the circumstances I didn't understand rather than judging the circumstances themselves in light of Your character. It has only been through my daily time in Your Word and through communication with You that I realized this. Thank You for bringing me through this trial with better knowledge of You and for how dearly You love and cherish me.

Thursday, July 29, 2004

LORD, I HAVE realized that the fear of never having a child is an obstacle in my life. As much as I want to trust that Your plan is perfect, I still doubt it and let the fear creep into my heart. I want to relinquish the fear of never having a child to You. Work in my heart to allow me to truly let go of this fear and all the worries connected to it. Instead, enable me to use that time and energy to glorify You and shine forth Your love with a heart free of anxiety and "what ifs."

Tuesday, August 3, 2004

ONE DAY I feel so secure in my faith, and by the next day, I have lost perspective and let the old anxieties creep back in. I spend precious time thinking about how things could be different rather than thanking You with every breath for the blessings in my life. Instead of looking forward to what You have planned for me, I start thinking things would have been better if hadn't miscarried and had our children to hold. I change my tune so quickly. Help me to keep my eyes fixed on You and to concentrate on the work You have for me to do.

Friday, August 6, 2004
(John 11)

I CAN SEE SO much of Martha in me. She was looking back to what could have happened if Jesus had gotten there earlier, and Jesus answered her by saying that if she believed she would see the glory of God. So often in my life I question the direction in which You are leading me, but You always answer back in such a way that I can no longer doubt Your divine plan. If Jesus had come and healed Lazarus, it would have been the expected action. Instead, by raising Lazarus from the dead, He displayed the true magnificence of His power and glory. When I ask my "if only" questions, I have to remember that I am Your child and believe that You have an "if" to answer back with that is even more glorious than I could imagine.

Monday, August 9, 2004

ONCE AGAIN I am feeling the effects of the fertility drugs on my body. I am not feeling like myself, and I am finding it hard to concentrate on things. My time with You is also being affected—that is just one more thing that upsets me each day. Once again I hope that this is all worth it in the end. I know that the odds are not as good since we are using frozen embryos this time, but I still have hope in Your power, Father. I pray that You will help me to keep my emotions in check and will daily remind me that You are working out Your perfect plan.

Wednesday, August 11, 2004

FATHER, SO OFTEN I displace my anger with You onto others, especially Lee. When I am going through a period when I am very upset with You for making us wait for a family, I will lash out at Lee or at my friends who are pregnant. Many times I won't verbalize it, but I will feel it in my heart, and I am sure that my actions show it. I look at other people who have children but take them for granted, or those who complain about every little thing during pregnancy, and I want to scream. I would do anything to know the joy of being a mother or to feel the miracle of life moving inside me, so it is extremely hard to listen to complaints or criticisms from others. I get angry with You, but instead of dealing with that, I displace that anger onto others. At other times, I get mad at myself for the way I handle something or for losing sight of what is truly important, and Lee often takes the brunt of that anger. Afterwards I feel so awful, because he is trying so hard to be supportive, and instead of appreciation he gets an earful of ugly words. Please help me to recognize my anger, either with You or myself, and deal with it rather than making others feel the pain.

Monday, August 16, 2004

*L*ORD, I KNOW there is a reason that You have me in this place right now, aching for a child. The valleys I enter are times of training under Your direction. You put me here. You keep me safe here. You teach me lessons while I wait, and ultimately, You will bring me out in Your time. In the midst of my trial, You are watching over me and giving me Your love so freely. I can travel this journey gracefully with You by my side. I know that I will stumble along the way. Please keep picking me up, brushing me off, and leading me with Your hand in mine.

Tuesday, August 17, 2004

I HAD AN ULTRASOUND today, and they found that I have another ovarian cyst, which means more waiting. Why does this keep happening? I am so frustrated because my body doesn't seem to work like it is supposed to. I know that the fertility medication is making me more anxious and emotional, so this seems more overwhelming than it really should be. I want this to work and to have the final outcome be a child, but I just have a feeling that it isn't going to. I don't know why, and I feel like I should believe that it will until I am proved wrong, but I just have that little feeling in my gut that this isn't our time. Please give me patience to wait out this cyst and a positive attitude going forward.

Thursday, August 19, 2004

I HAVE BEEN THINKING back today over the last four years and all that has happened. I still long for my prayer to be answered for a child, but I think I can finally embrace this burden as a blessing. I wouldn't be the person I am today without all the setbacks and disappointments I have had to face. As hard as it has been, I can't close my eyes and ignore the blessings that have come from it. You brought me to a point where I had no choice but to fall on my knees and cry out to You for the strength to go on. Lee and I are closer than ever, and our marriage has been strengthened as we both have grown in our faith. Thank You for standing by my side and making it all okay.

Tuesday, August 24, 2004

I HAVE ASKED YOU the question, "why me?" so many times, Lord, especially in the last four years. Why do I have to be the one to suffer through infertility? Why am I the one who has to deal with all the physical and emotional issues of two miscarriages? I have come a long way in trusting You since I consistently got back into Your Word and surrounded myself with encouraging, Christian friends. It is still a struggle every day, though, and the same nagging questions still live in my head.

Monday, August 30, 2004

GOD, AS I look around this world I have realized that there are things You made that seem imperfect or strange to us but that serve a purpose somehow. You made the giraffe with a strange-looking, long, skinny neck, and sometimes You make puppies with crooked tails. We tend to want to change anything that doesn't fit into our idea of "normal." You make things crooked for a reason, and in many cases, we don't have the power to straighten them out, which is for the best. When I am happy and things are going well in my life, I need to stop and enjoy the moment, just be happy. When things aren't going so well, I must remember that Your hand is in that somehow too. You have a reason for putting me into every situation, and I should keep my eyes wide open so that I won't miss Your presence there. You know what I need so much better than I do. Help me to trust that.

Wednesday, September 1, 2004

I HAD ANOTHER VISIT from You, Father, during my yoga/Pilates class today. The music during the meditation time had the sound of ocean waves crashing onto the beach, so that naturally took my mind to the most beautiful beach I could think of. I was just standing on the shore looking out at the sunset, and then I saw You walking toward me on the water. I watched You in amazement, thinking, "Is He coming to talk to me?" You walked onto the beach, and I ran into Your arms and was instantly enveloped in an embrace that felt so familiar and complete. You held me for a while, and then You looked me in the eyes and reminded me that You will always take care of me. You said, "I have even greater things in store for You than You know. I will always be by Your side. I love You, my child." You walked back out onto the water and turned around to smile at me again before You disappeared over the horizon. Thank You so much for giving me these moments with You. I am filled with joy and peace, and I can't wait to see what Your plan is for me.

Friday, September 3, 2004
(Habakkuk 3:17–19)

Though I don't have a child...
Though this IVF cycle has been delayed...
Though I feel uncertain about my future...
Though I feel inadequate because my body isn't working right...

"YET, I WILL rejoice in the Lord, I will be joyful in God my Savior! The Sovereign Lord is My Strength!"

I have learned all over again about Your sovereignty and Your power, and I have felt Your love so completely. I have learned that above all else I must trust in You. I can't see the future, and I can't change the past, so I must live in the present, continually searching for ways to glorify You.

Wednesday, September 8, 2004

AM I TRULY following You, Lord? Some days I let other things get in the way of my time with You, but I can honestly say that I want Your will for my life, whatever it may be. It has been a journey to get to a place where I can say that with confidence. For so long I didn't want to give up control, and there are still so many days when I fight the urge to take it back, but at least now I realize that giving it up is what You require of me. Your ways may seem more difficult, but in the end they will bring about the most blessings in my life. I know that somehow this period of waiting is what is best for me.

Friday, September 10, 2004

I AM TRYING TO keep my mind full of positive thoughts, as I am bedridden after my IVF transfer today. There is so much time to ponder all the possibilities when all I can do is lie flat on my back. I ultimately must put my trust in Your plan and pray for patience and peace as I wait for the results. I hope with all my might that this is finally our time to bring a child into this world. Hope is such a beautiful virtue and a wonderful thing to hang onto in the midst of the unknowns. Fill me to overflowing with the hope of Your promises and the peace of Your omniscience.

Monday, September 13, 2004
(JOHN 1:35–51; 9:35–41)

I CAN SEE THAT each of these readings is showing us how important it is to follow You and trust in Your guidance. This means not just saying that we follow You but honestly wanting in our hearts to do what is right and to listen closely for Your voice to guide us. For the past seven or eight months I have felt, more than I ever have before, like the path I am on is truly the right one, Your path. To bring all my concerns to You and just wait and listen for Your voice allows Your answer to fill me with a new sense of peace. Now I must keep my steps in time with Yours and keep my ear ever closer to Your heart so that I will know exactly what Your will reveals.

Tuesday, September 14, 2004

SOMETIMES I SEE so clearly how focused on this world I can become. For example, right now I am focused on waiting to hear if our IVF worked. I can't even keep my mind on You and Your Word today, which is the one thing that could take my anxieties away. No matter what happens, Your plan will be brought into the light, and I must know that is what is best for me. All my time spent worrying is wasted time. I must turn my eyes to You and find that still place where I can concentrate and know that You are the God in control. Your disciples seemed so much more focused on You than on the crazy things going on in the world around them. Was it easier for them because they had You there physically? Your Spirit is bright and alive within me, to guide me forward always—thank You.

Wednesday, September 15, 2004

YOU HAVE GIVEN me such a sense of peace since Friday. I am sure that I will still be sad and disappointed if I am not pregnant, but I have the assurance of knowing that what You have planned is so much better. I will need a large dose of strength no matter what the outcome. I will either need strength to know what to do next and move ahead, or strength to make it through the first trimester without worrying every minute. I want to be spiritually aware not spiritually blind. I believe You can do anything and that You always will do what is best for Your children.

Tuesday, September 21, 2004

(1 Kings 19:9b–18)

SO OFTEN I whine like Elijah is doing in these verses. I, just like Elijah, want to make sure You know my rough circumstances and repeat it every time I come into Your presence. Are You tired of hearing me cry out? Are You fed up with my frustration over not being a mother? I try to listen for You even in the gentle whisper, but do I miss You sometimes because I am too caught up in what is going on around me? I pray that You keep my eyes and ears open to hear You when You call me. Do not allow the circumstances in my life to consume me to the point where I am not following or listening to You.

Wednesday, September 22, 2004

I AM SO ANXIOUS this morning as I wait for my pregnancy test results. I want so badly for IVF to work this time, but Your will is what should be the most important thing to me. If I am not pregnant, then I must remember Your words to me during my exercise class a few weeks ago, "I have even greater things in store for You than You know. I will always be by Your side. I love You, my child." And if I am pregnant, then I must allow You to take all my worries and anxieties and just enjoy every moment. Right now I just want You to fill me with Your peace.

Friday, September 24, 2004
(Matthew 16:21–26)

LORD, I HAVE been on such a roller coaster ride of emotions over the last two days. I had convinced myself that I was pregnant, probably because of all the progesterone I am taking, but I found out that I really wasn't. Now we have another failed attempt at a family under our belt. I don't understand why Lee and I have to wait for a family. How do I even begin to get my arms around the idea that we may never have children of our own? Why us, when so many others have children they don't appreciate, little gifts from You that they don't realize are beautiful blessings? At Bible study yesterday I heard Your voice. I heard You speaking to me, calming my tattered heart, and reminding me that You have greater things in store for us. During the lesson, we talked about how the "follow me" invitation Jesus gives to his disciples means that we have to come up alongside You and walk through the cross with You. Your way often isn't the easy way, but it is always the best way. The trials we walk through allow us to have the testimony we need to bring others to You. I want so much to do Your will, so both Lee and I must pray and listen to discern what that is. Please guide us, hold us close, and enable us to bear this pain with grace.

Monday, September 27, 2004
(Matthew 13:1–23)

LORD, I SEE myself in each aspect of the parable of the farmer sowing his seed. I know there have been times when I heard but didn't understand because I let Satan snatch away what You put in my heart. I know there have been times when I have been renewed with joy over the gift of Your Son, but as soon as heartache came, I let that joy slip away. I know that there have been times when I have let the things of this world choke Your Word in my heart, which led me to make decisions that were not Your will for me, and many times those decisions went against Your commands. But, praise the Lord that there have been times when I have heard Your Word, understood it, and allowed it really to rule my life. I thank You for opening my heart to You, for allowing me to hear Your beautiful voice. In all my life, in all my struggles, I have never seen You more clearly or heard Your voice more strongly than through this latest, most heart-wrenching trial of longing for a child. Your ways amaze and humble me, Father. Allow me to always keep my eyes looking upward to my true home with You.

Tuesday, September 28, 2004
(John 12:20–26)

JOHN REMINDS ME again here of the true willingness we must have to lose our earthly lives to follow Christ. I have to be honest and tell You, Father, that this scares me. Am I strong enough to stand up for You in the face of losing my wonderful husband and family? It isn't so much the material things of this world that hold me back but my relationships with those I love. I want to experience Your honor because I serve Your Son, but at what price will it come in my life? I have let go of so much over the last few years that was getting in the way of our relationship. What more will You ask of me?

Wednesday, September 29, 2004

(MATTHEW 13:1–23)

FATHER, I SHOULD be so grateful that You have opened my ears and eyes. I should consider it a privilege to be still and listen for Your voice, Your wisdom. At times I have felt like it is such a burden on me to have to work so hard to know what it is You want me to do. But I am overwhelmed after reading in Matthew 13 that You have given me the ability to hear You and understand. I need to remember that I am so blessed to be able truly to walk in Your will, to follow Your perfect plan for my life. Help me to remember this in the midst of the waiting.

Friday, October 1, 2004

(PHILIPPIANS 3:12–4:1)

WHEN I THINK of pressing toward a goal as I read Philippians, my first thought is of an earthly goal, and I start questioning You, Father, about what goal I am to be pressing towards. Then, as I read it through more carefully a few more times, I understand that this goal is not earthly but heavenly. My goal should be to press on through this life, living out Christ's attributes to the world, and allowing others to see Christ in me as I keep my eyes heavenward, longing for my eternal home with You. I must die to myself daily, walk the road to the cross with Your Son daily, and live my life only for Christ, leaving the earthly goals behind.

Monday, October 4, 2004

(Exodus 33:12–23)

AS I READ about Moses here, I have a mixture of feelings. In a way it gives me comfort to hear You say, "My Presence will go with You, and I will give You rest" (v. 14). It takes a weight off my shoulders that I have been carrying concerning this decision of what to do about our future. But these same words of Yours also confuse me as I ponder what You are trying to tell me through it. What are we supposed to be going forth with that You will bless with Your Presence? Will You hide me in the cleft of a rock so that I can experience Your glory? Why did You do this for Moses? Calm my anxious thoughts, Father.

Tuesday, October 5, 2004

HEAVENLY FATHER, YOU know my heart, my longings and desires, my fears and confidences, my triumphs and failures. I know You see me struggling right now to know what Your will is for my life. I feel like I have been truly able to give this decision to You, for the first time. So why won't You answer me? I delight in knowing Your will and honestly want to do what You want me to do, but it isn't clear. Your Word says that if we honestly seek Your will, You will reveal it and bless us, but I don't hear You. Am I being impatient? Am I not listening well enough? Where are You, Lord? Please give me ears to hear and eyes to see the wonderful plans You have for me. Help me to be alert to Your words and that still, small voice.

Wednesday, October 6, 2004

(Exodus 33:12–23)

I HAVE BEEN DRAWN back to this passage so often this week. I have found such beauty in the words, but I am not sure exactly why. Maybe it is the intimate relationship with Moses that is revealed or the comfort of the words, "I am pleased with You and I know You by name" (v. 17). I feel that I have an intimate relationship with You, but there is something in this passage that I am longing for, almost jealous of. Maybe it is that Moses had a dialogue with You like I am hoping for. I want so desperately for You to tell me exactly what to do and for me to hear You clearly—or to tell You what I want and have You grant it because You find favor with me.

Friday, October 8, 2004

THERE IS SO much on my mind and heart as I write today, Father. I have been surrounded by so many teachings and lessons from Your Word in the last two days, which have only added to my confusion of what Your will is for my life right now. I long to climb into Your lap, lay my head on Your chest, hear Your heartbeat, and let my cares and worries melt away. I so vividly remember, as a child, climbing into bed at night and talking to You as my best friend, with a child's faith, feeling Your presence with me, and not second-guessing whether it was really You but believing it with all my heart. Oh, what wonderful talks we had. They were all about such simple things, but You listened like my thoughts were Your only concern. I don't know when that stopped, but I have come to miss that strong, simple faith. Now I try to complicate everything, and I wonder sometimes if You are really listening. I need a dose of that faith right now, to feel that close to You.

    I have gone back to Exodus 33 many times as I yearn for Your will. As Moses did, I want to say to You, "Now show me Your glory" (v.18). I long to see You pass by, to feel the breeze on my face as You come near. I am ready to come out of the cold, dark cleft in the rock so that Your glory and blessings can rain down on me. My heart is crying out to You to bless me, to take my hand and lead me to where I am supposed to go. Lord, I know and love Your Son, the ultimate Sacrifice, so I am now bound to You as a wife to her husband. I submit to Your ways, so now show me, guide me, and bring me into Your glory.

Holy Creator, You already know my children, and I am so ready to know them too. I beg You to show me the next step I am to take toward becoming a mother, which You have promised me. You knew all of my days before I was even born, so You also know the days of the children You will bless us with. What are they like, Lord? Do they smile and laugh a lot as I imagine they will? Do they have a deep knowledge and love of You like I pray they will? What will they accomplish in their lives? What do they look like? I can't wait to meet them. Please bring them soon, Father, and prepare my heart for their arrival into this world. I wish I knew how much longer Lee and I must walk this road of longing before Your promise is fulfilled, but I must rest in the knowledge that You will fill our empty arms at exactly the right time.

Monday, October 11, 2004

THANK YOU, FATHER, for speaking to me and calming my heart. On Friday I was so anxious and worked up about not being able to hear You, but You made it very obvious to me that right now I just need to come into Your presence. I need to let You take my burden and know that You are working out the details and circumstances of Your plan for my life. First, You gave me the "Guidance" devotion from *Come Away My Beloved*[4], calling me Your child and urging me to hear Your voice and follow only You. Then I happened to run across *My Utmost For His Highest*[5], which I hadn't read in quite a while, so I turned to the October 8th devotion. In its pages I heard You telling me to "come" and ask the Holy Spirit to remove anything hindering me from truly doing that. Without even knowing it, I have put obstacles in between You and me so that Your voice isn't clear to me. Friday night Lee and I went to a Bible study, and the instructor talked all about the Holy Spirit, confirming for me again that all I need to do is "come." This morning I opened *Come Away My Beloved*[4] again, and there were the words I needed to really cement Your voice in my heart ("On the Waters of Sorrow"). Thank You so much for breaking through that barrier I had put up in my mind, thinking You were trying to tell me to do some grand task that I wasn't grasping, when all You really want from me right now is my attention, my love, and my adoration. Help me to continue just coming into Your presence, knowing that You will reveal what I am to do in Your time, not mine. I ask that Your Holy Spirit continue to remove the barriers that keep me from You.

Tuesday, October 12, 2004

(John 21:15–22)

THIS PASSAGE MAKES me realize how often You have to tell me something or ask me a question before I finally realize it's You, Lord. How many times did You have to tell me just to come into Your presence before it really sank in? I know it was definitely more than three times. Why is that? I want to be able to hear Your voice the first time and know without a doubt that it is You. Thank You for being so persistent, for driving the point home until I finally hear and see. Help me to know Your voice above all the other chatter of this world. Tune my ears so that I can hear You in the midst of a roaring crowd.

Wednesday, October 13, 2004
(John 21:15–22)

FATHER, AS I read John 21:18, I feel as if You are describing me. When I was younger I did what I wanted to do and didn't lean on You for guidance and direction. Now You are leading me to places I don't want to go, but I am much more willing to follow You. I see myself again later in the passage when Peter asks, "Lord, what about him [John]?" (v. 21). I compare myself with others all the time. Sometimes it is because of what they have, like children, or what I think is a stronger, more abiding faith in You. As You told Peter, "What is that to You? You must follow me" (v. 22). Help me to keep my eyes on following You rather than comparing my lot with others.

Monday, October 18, 2004

(John 14)

VERSE 28 OF John 14 jumped out at me as I read it this morning. Jesus tells His disciples that they should be happy He is leaving them because the Father is greater, but I tend to think it would be easier for me if I had You physically here with me. Is that wrong? I do feel Your strength, Your Spirit in me, but sometimes I long for a visible presence. However, as I think about this, I would not want to be here on earth without Your Spirit living in me, which the disciples didn't have. So, maybe I have sorted this out by thinking on paper, letting Your Spirit move in me. The peace that comes with having Your Spirit is stronger than everything, and one day I will see You. Thank You for this time, this revelation through Your Spirit.

Tuesday, October 19, 2004
(John 15)

THE PASSAGES THAT stand out to me here are those that claim that if I remain in You I will have whatever I wish (v. 7, 16). You know my wish to be a mother, and I am spending more time in Your Word, in prayer, with thoughts of You than ever before, yet my wishes have not been granted. Why? What more do I need to do or learn before I can become a mother? I know Your plans for me are beautiful and perfect, but right now these verses frustrate me rather than help me. Please give me comfort and wisdom to discern Your voice.

Monday, October 25, 2004
(Deuteronomy 30:6, 10–20)

THE IDEA THAT we have the choice of life or death in this lifetime and some choose death is hard to believe. I want to obey You, Lord, to choose life in You and hold it close to my heart. I often act like Your commands are far off and not clear, but really, they are in my heart. If I search, there I will find them and know how I am to act in obedience to You. I want to have descendants, children to pass this beautiful gift to. I believe You will grant me that as promised. It is just the "how" that escapes me right now. I choose life, Father! I choose You and Your ways in my life.

Tuesday, October 26, 2004

(2 Corinthians 4:5–18)

SOMETIMES I CANNOT fathom all that You have done for me, Father. Your love is so powerful and mighty. As it says in 2 Corinthians 4:6, "For God…made his light shine in our hearts to give us the light of knowledge of the glory of God in the face of Christ." You have given us all we need and more so that we will be comfortable putting our trust completely in You. I tend to get caught up in and focused on this temporal place and the demands of this physical life. Instead I need to have an eternal perspective. The grief and fears over not being a mother on this earth seem so much smaller and less burdensome when I look at them with the correct mindset, an eternal one. I have babies waiting for me in heaven right now. How beautiful!

Wednesday, October 27, 2004

BY CHOOSING YOU, I have chosen life. This is such a hopeful thought. You, Your Word, and the reassurance of Your return live in my heart. It is amazing that at times You feel far away, but really You are always here. I think at those times it is me who is far away, trying to exercise my own control or letting circumstances dictate my feelings for You. I become so frustrated when I don't know what You have planned for me, but You are always there, working out the details while I throw myself a big "pity party." I must wait for You with expectation rather than impatience, since what You have in store will bring the most amazing blessings.

Tuesday, November 2, 2004

(ROMANS 8:1–17; EPHESIANS 4:17–24)

THESE PASSAGES SPEAK so strongly of a clear difference in our mindset once the Spirit comes to dwell in us. I truly long for an undivided mind, especially right now. I want my mind and heart to be able to know without a doubt what is of this world and what is from You. Is that too much to ask, Father? I want the wisdom You willingly give, and I want to know Your heart. What do You have in store for us? What is around the next bend? Will it be more heartache, or finally the answer to our prayers? Help me to continue to wait with expectation, and I ask that You bestow on Lee and me the wisdom to discern Your will.

Wednesday, November 3, 2004

(Ephesians 4:17–24)

HOW AMAZING THAT the new self we put on when we accept Your Son, Jesus Christ, into our lives causes us to be "created to be like God in true righteousness and holiness" (v. 24). Some days I feel so far from being that new self. I get weighed down with worries, busyness, and the demands of this world. I know those are the moments when what I need most is quiet time with You, but that is also often the time when going to You is the last thing I want to do. My devotion today talked about how we must be intercessors, spending that quiet time with You in prayer, or the seeds You have sown will dry up. Help me to be that new self more often and to crawl into Your lap willingly on a regular basis.

Friday, November 5, 2004

*D*URING MY BIBLE study today we discussed what it means to have an undivided mind. The instructor encouraged us to visualize actually handing our mind over to You. I think the concept is wonderful, but to actually do it seems abstract somehow. I prayed about it after the lesson and visualized standing before Your throne with my mind in my hands, offering it to You. How do I know if I truly gave it up or not? I am sure that it is a gradual process and something I will have to do quite often as I start trying to take control of it again. The instructor also gave us a visual aid for what to do with all the thoughts that enter our head. Each thought knocks at the door of our mind, and we will waste our energy trying to hold the door closed to the thoughts that we don't think should be there. Instead, we should let all our thoughts in and then choose to either entertain the thought or escort it right out the back door to the foot of the cross. I think this will be very helpful to me since I am such a visual learner. The mind is the battleground of the soul, and we must protect it from the blows of Satan. I feel like often I think too much about certain things and then end up more confused than ever. I am feeling lately like this decision between IVF and adoption is a battle being waged in my mind. My heart wants to follow You and have another chance at a child of our own. Is this a contradiction or not? I feel the two choices whirling around in my head all the time, and I want so badly to have peace about one or the other. Take my mind, Father, so that I can have the mind of Christ in its place.

Monday, November 8, 2004
(Psalm 96)

I DON'T THINK IT is a coincidence that Psalm 96 has been put before me twice today. David writes with such passion about praising You and worshiping You with a right heart. Verse 1 says specifically that we are to "sing to the Lord a new song." What is that new song for me, Lord? Am I overlooking something, or are You wanting me to concentrate on worshiping You in a new way? Is there a new song that should be or will be on my lips soon? So many questions today…

Tuesday, November 9, 2004

HEAVENLY FATHER, I think You have finally gotten through to me. I believe that You want me to wait right now. I don't know for how long or for what reason, but I am feeling like You just want us to listen right now. I think it took me a while to get to this point, because it wasn't the answer I wanted to hear. I wanted a clear sign from You to either do IVF or adopt, and I allowed myself to get frustrated because I wasn't hearing one of those two things. Waiting seems like the hardest thing to do right now, but I truly believe that is what You want. You know what lies a few months down the road for us, and I must trust in that with all my heart.

Wednesday, November 10, 2004

(Psalm 95:1–7)

FATHER, OVER AND over You have calmed my heart and settled my mind with Your command to "Come." Now here it is again in Psalm 95, and once again, it is a comfort. Since our last IVF, Lee and I have been feeling like we are lost, not knowing what You want us to do. But You have kept bringing me Scripture verses that say to "come into Your presence," "come to me," or just "come." These commands have made me feel peaceful for a time. Then I have allowed the things of this world to seep in, and I have surrendered that peace. After finally realizing yesterday that You want us to wait right now, I am better able to come to You and remain peaceful.

Friday, November 12, 2004

FATHER, YOU HAVE filled me with so much lately. I don't understand what it all means yet, but I am hoping that when the time is right, You will reveal it to me. I think I have made a connection between the first verse of Psalm 96 (the "new song" portion that stood out to me as I was reading it the other day) and Deuteronomy 8:3, which is a portion of a passage that I have gone back to so many times before. Deuteronomy 8:3 says, "He humbled you, causing you to hunger and then feeding you with manna, which neither you nor your fathers have known, to teach you that man does not live on bread alone but on every word that comes from the mouth of the Lord." This passage has always intrigued me and called to me in a way since I first read it. In Bible study yesterday we discussed the "new song" portion of Psalm 96, and the instructor said that it means "something beyond what we have known before," which made me think of the Deuteronomy passage. I feel that these two verses are connected somehow (although I don't know how) and that You are about to bring about something wonderful. It makes my heart expectant, which is a wonderful feeling. I can't wait to see what You have in store for us!

Monday, November 15, 2004

(Psalm 27)

LORD, THANK YOU for all Your reassurances today. You have told me over and over again that You long for me to just come into Your presence, and over the last week that is really setting into my heart and my mind. This psalm is such a comfort to me as I ponder that. The idea of living with You, seeing Your face, and studying at Your feet fills me with overwhelming love for You. All this I can have if I willingly come into Your presence daily and strengthen our relationship. At the end of the psalm You have another reminder for us to wait with IVF right now (v. 14). Thank You for bringing me to this point, Father, for bringing me closer to Your heart.

Tuesday, November 16, 2004
(Romans 11:33–12:2)

FATHER, YOU HAVE placed Romans 12:1–2 before me so many times in the last few weeks that I feel like I should be getting some profound message from it. What jumps out at me as I read the whole passage is the contrast: how wonderful, merciful, almighty, wise, etc., You are and that all You ask of me in return is to give my ordinary life to You as a sacrifice. How unbalanced that scale is! My life, full of its sins, wrong thoughts, and selfish actions, is nothing in comparison to Your gift, and yet You want it, and I fight giving it up. Why should I fight giving You something broken in return for Your wholeness? I love the *Message*[6] translation of 12:1–2: "So here's what I want you to do, God helping you: Take your everyday, ordinary life—your sleeping, eating, going-to-work, and walking-around life—and place it before God as an offering. Embracing what God does for you is the best thing you can do for him. Don't become so well-adjusted to your culture that you fit into it without even thinking. Instead, fix your attention on God. You'll be changed from the inside out. Readily recognize what he wants from you, and quickly respond to it. Unlike the culture around you, always dragging you down to its level of immaturity, God brings the best out of you, develops well-formed maturity in you." This helps me to see what a living sacrifice really is—just my everyday, ordinary life as an offering to You. Take it, Father, and use me as You will. I truly want to give my heart and mind over to You, to do Your will, to bring a smile to Your face. Is there more You want me to get from this, or do I stumble across it so often because You are just reminding me of what will bring me the most blessing in my life? It is becoming obvious that You want my full attention, and I will come to You daily with expectation of what You have planned for me.

Tuesday, November 30, 2004

FATHER, I HAVE missed You. My parents have been here visiting for Thanksgiving and just left this morning. I loved having them here and spending so much quality time together, so seeing them go was hard for me. I decided the only place to go to make the lonely ache diminish was into Your Word. I have been so blessed to be surrounded by Christian teaching and parenting my whole life. Your Word has always been important to me, but in the last few years I have been especially thirsty for Your words and Your guidance. I think this thirst has allowed me to acquire an even greater appreciation for having Your words available to me anytime, rather than taking the Bible on the shelf for granted. I say this now, but there are still often days when I fall into the attitude of *having* to sit with You rather than *wanting* to. You are waiting right here for me everyday. Help me to meet You with longing in my heart.

Wednesday, December 1, 2004

(2 Timothy 3:14–4:5; James 1:22–27)

A FEW DIFFERENT THINGS jumped out at me as I read these passages this morning. In 2 Timothy, I keep coming back to verse 15 about knowing the Holy Scriptures from infancy. This reminds me that I need to have faith like a child as You ask of me. Also, in James 1:27 it says that the religion You consider pure is caring for orphans and widows. Of course, the word orphan jumps off the page and into my heart because of the inevitable decisions Lee and I have ahead of us. I am feeling anxious about it again, which could either be my human impatience, or it could be You nudging me forward. I honestly don't know which direction to go. Does that mean that it doesn't matter, that either choice would be fine? Or does it mean that I am just not hearing You? I pray that You will either ease my heart to continue waiting, or open my ears to Your voice. Another good friend told me she is pregnant today, and an aquaintance who is pregnant talked about her pregnancy constantly while we were together today. I now have no friends here who don't have children or aren't pregnant, which makes me sad. Instead of taking me out of situations where I will be surrounded by babies or talk of motherhood, I feel like I am being suffocated by everything and anything related to being a mother. Why God?? All I can do is ask You for strength to make it through these difficulties by remembering that it is when I am weak that I am strong.

Monday, December 6, 2004

(Psalm 119)

I LOVE HOW YOU speak to me, Father. In the rush of the holidays it seems that my time with You gets put at the bottom of the list, but today I decided that, no matter how much needs to get done, sitting down with Your Word is most important. As I read Psalm 119 I felt like You were telling me that, as long as I am not going against Your laws, You will fulfill Your promise to me. Maybe that's just what I want to hear, but as I sat down to read I was prepared for any word from You, and I feel like this might be just a little morsel of spiritual food for my soul. I need to continue listening to You before making a decision. It was so comforting to be near You today. Thank You…

Friday, December 10, 2004

(Psalm 121)

FATHER, THANK YOU so much for filling me up today as I read Your Word. I so easily forget that the Bible contains Your very thoughts and words. You will always meet me there if I come with an open heart. I was in such pain this morning, but You have strengthened me during our time together. I got my period last night, which explains some of the sadness. Each month when it arrives it is another reminder that children are just out of reach for us, and it makes me feel like a failure. My sadness over that is magnified by the fact that the due date of my last pregnancy is approaching (Dec. 13th). I have spent a good amount of time lately thinking about what could have been, and it makes my arms feel even more empty than usual. All the people around me are blessed with children or are full of excitement over their pregnancies, and some days it is such a struggle to show happiness for them when I am dying inside. They so easily have what Lee and I long for constantly.

    I also had high hopes for this month because of something that happened a few weeks ago. Lee and I were at a Bible study, and the teaching was on the power of healing. After the lesson, a large group of us formed a circle, and the leader, who knows about our struggles with infertility, asked me to sit in the middle of the circle. Everyone laid their hands on me and prayed for my womb to be opened and healed. I felt a tightening in my abdomen as they were praying, so I was hopeful that it had worked. I held onto that hope for weeks, believing that Your work could be accomplished through this healing and, of course, wanting it to be true. So last night I felt my heart breaking again as I realized that it didn't work, and I felt so defeated. I can't even begin to understand Your plan in all this, Lord. I know You have one, a perfect one, but from down here it looks and feels like I am being asked to carry a burden more difficult to bear than I could have imagined. The only way I have made it this far is with Your strength, patience, and love for me. I didn't want to sit down with Your Word today, but when I did, there You were in Psalm 121 telling me that You will protect me and let no harm befall me. Then I opened *Come Away My Beloved*[4] and read the "Give Me a Drink" devotion, which You also used to speak to my wounded heart. One sentence in this devotion was exactly what I needed to hear today. It said, "Miss anything else but do not miss my voice." I need to hear You clearly, Father. I need to know which path is the right one, which one is yours. I second-guess my purpose every month when I'm not pregnant. Guide my steps and open my ears. Give me strength to persevere, knowing Your plan for my life is utterly perfect and will bring me the most blessing.

Monday, December 13, 2004
(1 Samuel 1)

FATHER, I AM struggling today with a sadness that feels like it is consuming me. My mind is focused on sad thoughts of self-pity. I am allowing the "what-ifs" and "whys" to creep in. What if I hadn't miscarried nine months ago? Why is this happening to me? Why is it so easy for everyone else in my life to have children? Then once again I reluctantly sat down for some time with You, and I feel Your strength filling me up and choking out the sadness and selfishness. I started reading 1 Samuel today not knowing what I was in for. It starts with the story of Hannah and her struggles and heartaches in wanting a child. I know You wanted me to read this story today, and I felt a warm feeling start to grow inside me as I began reading because I realized that You had hand-picked this reading just for me when I needed it the most. I have felt for a long time now that You have closed my womb as You did Hannah's, waiting for the perfect time to bring our children into this world. The explanation of Hannah being irritated by Elkanah's other wife, Peninnah, because she provoked her, brings so many feelings to the surface. People so often say things to Lee and me that are hard to take or hurtful. Usually they mean well and don't even know that what they have said breaks our hearts or irritates us, but it still does. The way Hannah weeps as she prays to You makes me feel so close to her. I want to reach out and comfort her, because I have prayed those prayers and know exactly how her heart aches. So often I have fallen at

Your feet in tears, wanting answers but still knowing deep in my heart that Your ultimate plan was in motion. As I read about her promise to You, I thought back to all the times I have cried out in desperation or prayed specific things. It made me realize again that one of the prayers I have consistently offered up to You has been that You would bless me with children that I could raise to know and love You completely. You have taught me so much along this journey, so maybe the waiting and learning is an answer to my prayer. By learning more about You, I can better teach my children the things they will need to know to make their relationship with You a priority. I am just being too impatient, rather than moving out of the way so that You can accomplish what I asked of You.

Tuesday, December 14, 2004

(Romans 10:8–17)

FATHER, HERE IS another passage You have put before me about evangelizing. I think I am finally getting Your message, and most importantly, I am finally ready to do what You want of me. As I continue in Your Word each day, I believe more and more that working to compile my journals is what You want of me as Your servant. You took so many people in the Bible and had them do things that they didn't think they could do, and You used their work to glorify You. I believe You want me to do the same. I am not a writer, but I have felt the emotions and walked the painful journey of infertility with my hand in Yours. I want to be the picture of beautiful feet bringing Your good news to others.

Wednesday, December 15, 2004
(John 15:1–11)

FATHER, BECAUSE OF the encouragement and strength I have gained from You and Your Word this week, I can say that I believe this whole painful process of waiting for a child has been a pruning that I needed. I am being pruned so that I can bear more fruit. Pruning is a cutting back, which I think is Your way of not letting us become too full of pride over what we have accomplished. We bear fruit and start to become proud, so You cut us back by putting trials in our lives so that we remember where our strength and gifts come from. Then we are able to go out and bear more fruit by using our experiences in those trials to help others. I wasn't prepared four years ago to be the mother I truly want to be or the mother You want me to be. I needed to be brought down to my knees, crying out to You for help and comfort. It was only through that pain that I was able to turn my life back to being focused on You, taking time to be with You every day, learning so much more about You. This I can pass on to my children, making me a better mother than I would have been. Once again, thank You for filling me up.

Thursday, December 16, 2004

(Romans 10:8–17)

ALL THAT I have read today is swirling around in my head and heart, not only the passage from Romans but also the *Come Away My Beloved*[4] devotion, "You Cannot Weary My Love." The thought from my devotion that You want to hear my voice almost took my breath away. I concentrate so much on trying to make sure I listen for Your voice that I have never thought about Your wanting to hear mine. I guess it wouldn't be a personal relationship without two-way communication though, would it? In reading Romans, I was overcome with awe at how Paul explains the ease of having You come into our lives. We just have to call out, and You are waiting to answer. Your love is amazing and complete, Father. Thank You for loving me and wanting to hear my voice.

Friday, December 17, 2004
(John 15:1–11)

FATHER, AS I read Your Son's words today in John, it made me think about how soft I am. Jesus endured so much for me when He was here on earth, but I allow my pain to be so all-consuming and feel cheated and upset when things don't go my way. My time here in this world is so small compared to an eternity with You, and while I am here, I must fight the good fight, for You, with courage. I am blessed with so much, but I seem to forget that at times—I let my worry and pain overwhelm me. I must keep Your Word in my heart for times like that so that I can recall what You have to say about it: "Do not be anxious about anything, but in everything, by prayer and petition, with thanksgiving, present your requests to God. And the peace of God, which transcends all understanding, will guard your hearts and your minds in Christ Jesus. Finally, brothers, whatever is true, whatever is noble, whatever is right, whatever is pure, whatever is lovely, whatever is admirable—if anything is excellent or praiseworthy—think about such things" (Philippians 4:6–8). This will allow me to get back on the right track and get my mind in the right place. I also must remember that Jesus is the Vine, You are the Gardener, and we are the branches. I am here, we are all here, to bear fruit. Even though we do bear fruit at times, we will still need to be pruned, which is painful but necessary, so that we can be even more fruitful in the future. Help me, Lord, to keep Your Word in my heart so that I can lean on it, call on it, and use it in all areas of my life.

Tuesday, January 4, 2005
(ROMANS 10:8–17)

THIS READING FROM Romans reminds me again how important Your Word is. We all need it to navigate through this life, yet we toss it aside so easily. We say things like, "I'll do it tomorrow. I'm just too busy today." We so easily discard the map that will guide us through all the things on our to-do list. Why is that? I am sure that Satan loves it when we do this. By ignoring the one thing we could use to fight against him, we are essentially opening the door to our lives and inviting Satan in. Keep me focused on being in Your Word daily, Father, and remind me how important it is in my life. I find myself putting the Word aside when I am sad or disappointed. It gives me an excuse to wallow in my self-pity, to feel sorry for myself, and to be jealous of all my friends that have children. I know that if I open up the Bible, You will point out to me why I shouldn't be upset or angry, which should comfort me, but at times it intimidates me. So I find other things to fill the time and tell myself that those things are just more important right now than sitting down with the Word. When I do finally come back to it, I am refreshed. You hold up Your end of the bargain every time by being there whenever I open up Your Book, but I fail You so often by not even coming. Forgive me, cleanse me, and guide me home to You again.

Wednesday, January 5, 2005

I MUST BEGIN TO make an extra effort in my relationship with You, Lord. I must go beyond the "follow me" command of a new Christian and walk with You. This means dying to self and living each moment for You. It means letting go of my desire for children, as much as that is in my ability to do, and living out Your Word and Your instructions so those around me will see You shining forth from me. So many people know about our situation, and if they could see me as a joyful person in the midst of my longing, it might make them ask why. Give me the boldness to say, with conviction, "It's Jesus!"

Friday, January 7, 2005
(John 13:1–17)

*I*N BIBLE STUDY yesterday we talked about Your Word and what it does for us. I loved the idea that every time we read Your Word You are washing our feet, cleansing us of our sin. Our bodies are always clean if we have accepted You as our Savior, but our feet get dirty as we walk in this world. We need Your Word to cleanse our feet and send us off again as lights to those around us. Your Word also sanctifies and equips us; without it we would be floundering through our days. Help me to remember what a treasure it is to have Your words available to guide me. I am a vessel that You want to use. How, Father? As I look at myself and my life, I wonder how I can be of service to You. I believe that writing a book using my journals may be part of what You have in store for my journey. I pray that You will open me up and pour in all I need to know to do this task well and in a way that glorifies You and draws others to You. I feel something in the air—maybe it's excitement for what is to come. Only You know the future, and I must be confident that it is all for my good. Humble me, Lord, and envelop me in Your arms of love and strength.

Tuesday, January 11, 2005

FATHER, I WAS brought to tears today, as usual, when I read my devotion from *Come Away My Beloved*[4] ("Household Salvation"). I once again felt like it was a personal letter straight from You to me. It completely summed up Your love for me, and then it said that one of Your promises is that **all** those in my household will be saved. It went on to say that my faith would be turned to sight, and my heart would rejoice over what will come to pass. You will do wonderful work, and we will praise You together as a family! It gave me such a sense of excitement and expectation of what Your plan contains for my life. What a wonderful feeling! I tend to look at the future as being tinged with sadness. I dwell on the negative, thinking our lives will never be filled with children and a happy family of our own. My devotion has renewed and refreshed me, and it has given me new energy to tackle this obstacle You have set before me. Lord, I ask that Your Spirit will come upon me and allow me to do all that I need to do so that Your will is carried out. This will only happen if I am allowing You to steer the ship. I ask for strength, perseverance, and guidance as I embark on this call to my heart.

Wednesday, January 12, 2005

(1 Peter 1:13–2:12)

I LOVE THE *MESSAGE*[6] Bible translation of this 1 Peter passage. It talks about how our lives should be shaped by God's life, "a life energetic and blazing with holiness," and that "your life is a journey you must travel with a deep consciousness of God." I want this in my life. I want to be so full of You that there is no doubt when people look into my eyes that I am in love with You, Father. I want You to be forever on my mind and in my heart so that every decision has Your stamp of approval all over it. I want my actions to show the world what Jesus is like, although it is just a glimpse.

Thursday, January 13, 2005

I FOUND OUT YESTERDAY that Josh and Ginny are expecting another baby. Again, a part of me is so excited to have another niece or nephew, but the other part of me is jealous and hurt. These feelings that I thought I had conquered come bubbling up to the surface, and I am paralyzed with confusion and bitterness. I want to be a mother. I want to be pregnant and know what it feels like to have a life moving inside of me. I see so many people that seem (from the outside at least) to have the exact life they want, and it causes feelings of jealousy to rise in me. It makes questions run through my head like: "Does God think we wouldn't be good parents?"; "Is there something I've done to deserve being denied a child?"; "Am I less of a Christian than they are?" I have to ask You to fill me with the love I should have for these people, Lord. Give me the strength to smile and genuinely offer a hand of love through my pain. Show me how to fight the temptation to be jealous, angry, and hard toward those I currently have difficulty reaching out to. I may never understand, this side of heaven, why others have so easily been given the one thing I long for every day of my life. It is only through You that I will be able to fight these ugly feelings. Help me to love rather than envy, embrace rather than push away, help rather than hurt, and most of all, find a piece of You in everyone.

Friday, January 14, 2005
(1 Samuel 13)

FATHER, I FEEL as if You are trying to get something across to me today, another message of "wait." I am still unsure if it means wait on IVF or wait on getting started with adoption or both. For some reason, I don't feel like it is a long-term message but that You want me to wait on something that will happen soon. My devotion today said, "To be almost in the perfect will of God is to miss it completely."[4] I want to be smack dab in the middle of Your perfect will for my life. 1 Samuel 13 explains how Saul grew impatient waiting for Samuel, so Saul took matters into his own hands. This brought great consequences to him because he was disobeying Your commands. Am I being impatient? Is four and a half years not long enough? What am I to wait for? Help me to see each step on this journey. Help me to know what choice is in agreement with Your glorious, perfect plan. Make me an instrument of Your Word, pliable in Your hand so I can bring about all You want of me. In moments of clarity, when the pain is not quite so acute, I am very aware of what my purpose is on this earth, which is to do Your work. Everything else, including having a child, is simply the extras of this life, not needs but desires of my own human heart.

Wednesday, January 19, 2005

I AM FEELING OVERWHELMED right now, Father. We have been waiting to hear from You, waiting to know how to proceed with adoption and/or IVF. In the meantime, we have found out that our insurance will cover 100% of IVF after we have paid a certain amount out-of-pocket. This, of course, got both Lee and me so excited about doing IVF again, and we both sensed that it may have been a sign from You about what to do. We no longer felt like we would be wasting the money You have blessed us with if it didn't work. We decided we would try it again in April after we are back from all our traveling. All this made me feel very at peace, so I thought it was Your will, but today as I read my devotion I felt like You were sending me a conflicting message to keep waiting. My devotion said, "When God gives a vision and darkness follows, wait. God will make you in accordance with the vision He has given if you will wait His time. Never try and help God fulfill His Word."[5] It also talked about how, when we are given a vision, You put us in the shadow of Your hand, and we must be still and listen. I feel that ever since You gave me the promise of bearing children I have listened, but now I am second-guessing what I thought was right. Give me clarity, Lord, and peace of mind.

Friday, January 21, 2005

FATHER, HELP MY unbelief. I believe that You are the One True God, that Your Son laid down His life as a sacrifice for my sins, but I find myself not believing Your promise to me of having children. I allow myself to get so upset over this decision about what to do next. I can know the answers to my questions if my heart is one with You. I can sit in Your presence and Your Spirit will fill me with understanding of Your Word if I will open my heart. Again, I cry, help my unbelief.

Wednesday, January 26, 2005

THERE IS NO doubt in my mind that I need to follow Your guidance, Father. I cannot let the influences and opinions of this world make our decision about our next steps toward having a family. The problem is I am so confused about what Your guidance actually is. The fact that our insurance will soon cover 100% of IVF takes away the financial worries, but is this what You want us to do? Is this how You want to bring about a miracle in our lives? Or is this the way of the world? By doing this, am I failing to believe that You can make it happen on Your own? By not doing it, am I failing to believe that You can do Your work through any means You choose? Lee really thinks we should do IVF again. Do You want me to follow his lead or stand up against it? I don't even really know if it is a decision between waiting and doing IVF or between IVF and adoption or among all three. My mind is a swirling mess of thoughts. I need Your guidance, Lord. I need to know the next step. Give Lee wisdom also so that we can make this decision together.

Thursday, January 27, 2005

I WAS AMAZED AT Bible study today as we learned about the power of Your grace. We try to claim so much for ourselves: that we chose You rather than the other way around, that we have the ability in us to be kind, patient, etc. But the only way we are able to do these things is through the grace You have supplied. You put the initial call on our hearts to come to You. We feel it, but our response happens because of the grace You pour out on us. Why is it so hard to let go of control? We want so much to be able to say we did it our way. Why? I pray, Lord, that You give me the desire to let go of all the ownership I try to take for things and, instead, hand it over to You. Help me to realize that Your grace is the only reason I am able to do anything good. Help me to remember to ask You for Your grace when I am in situations that I don't normally handle well. Keep this constantly on my heart and mind.

Tuesday, February 1, 2005

WE HAVE BEEN in Zurich visiting Josh, Ginny, and Tristan for the last few days. When I am able to spend time with my brother, I realize just how much I miss having him close by. I miss talking to him and catching up on his day-to-day life. Instead, we get glimpses into each other's lives, which isn't quite the same. I know that You have called him to be here to bring Your gospel to these kids, so I must be thankful for the time we do have and cherish every moment together. I also pray, Father, that You will take any jealous thoughts and feelings out of my heart. Allow me to put aside my heartache from not having a child and to embrace the fact that You have given Josh and Ginny the ability to have such a beautiful family. Give me strength to listen to the pregnancy details without feeling cheated or starting to cry. Give me the love and patience I need to bear this pain with grace and to show Your love through it.

Tuesday, February 8, 2005

(1 Kings 3:4–15)

YOU WERE SO pleased with Solomon when he asked for wisdom, and in turn, You blessed him abundantly. I must somehow learn to embrace this trial of infertility, knowing it will develop perseverance and make me more complete in You. Then I need to sincerely ask for wisdom and believe it will come. I must give my life up to You, Lord. In theory I know this, but I have had various reminders today of the need truly to die to self and to the things of this world. I know that I can never do this perfectly, but I must strive for it daily. I start to think sometimes that You won't bless me with a child until I get this all down perfectly, and I feel discouragement growing inside of me. Then I eventually realize that all I can do is open my heart daily to You and rely on Your strength to get it right. Why do You want to work so hard on me before I can be a mother? You don't seem to do this with others. They go about their lives without letting You in or thinking that they have this "Christian living thing" licked, but You still bless them with children. Is it because I want children so badly that this is the only way You can get through to me? I need to stop this questioning and instead focus on Your will for my life and what You want of me. Comparing my lot with others gets me nowhere and separates me from You. Keep me focused on You, Father, being one with You in spirit no matter what life has in store.

Wednesday, February 9, 2005
(1 Samuel 24)

I HAVE BEEN PONDERING all my various readings this morning before sitting down to put my thoughts on paper. I prayed so earnestly before I opened my books that You would give me clear direction about doing IVF again. I opened *Come Away My Beloved*[4] after praying, and it was full of references to the drought ending and the rain falling and new life springing forth. This made me think that moving forward is in Your plan. Then when I read 1 Samuel 24, I thought about how David honestly followed You and didn't try to make Your words fit the situation. Am I trying to make Your words fit my situation, Father? I know that *Come Away My Beloved*[4] is not Scripture, but I feel that You have used it before to speak to me. Neither choice in this decision violates Your laws. The question is whether or not it goes against Your will for our lives. I pray that Your Spirit will move in me, Lord, to let me know one way or another if this is the right step. Guide both Lee and me so that we can make a unified decision that pleases You.

Monday, February 14, 2005

(ROMANS 8:26–39; 1 CORINTHIANS 2:6–16)

THESE WORDS HAVE brought me comfort today—not necessarily answers, but definitely comfort. I allow myself to feel so alone and to think that all the weight of this IVF decision is on me. I don't know why I do this when I have a husband who willingly shares the responsibility and wants to help. I feel that if I make the wrong decision horrible things will happen, and I will look back and wish I had chosen differently. These passages remind me that the Holy Spirit is my intercessor. If I pray honestly from the heart for wisdom and understanding, Your Holy Spirit will take those prayers to the foot of Your throne. Then, knowing Your mind, the Spirit will answer with Your plan for my life. Yet sometimes I have a hard time discerning what is of You and what is of me. However, no matter what decision we make, You are ultimately in control. Even if I read things all wrong, nothing can separate me from the love You have for me. I really need to talk to Lee so I can better understand why he is feeling led to move ahead with IVF. I constantly struggle with why You would be leading him one way and me another. Please, Lord, bless our discussion and lead us to a conclusion together.

Tuesday, February 15, 2005

I AM STILL FEELING unsure, Father, wanting to hear Your voice so clearly so that there is no doubt in my mind what You want of me, of us. I talked to Lee for a while last night about all my mixed up thoughts. I told him that I felt like I was trying to read too much into everything I heard, read, or thought. I also asked him if we could make an effort to pray specifically about this together more regularly. We are each praying so faithfully on our own, but we don't take as much time as we should to pray about it together. He was very supportive, as usual, and made me feel that it was all right that I was confused right now. I pray that You will open his heart to hear You clearly also.

Wednesday, February 16, 2005

(1 Corinthians 2:6–16)

THANK YOU, FATHER, for Your reassurance today. I feel as if I am bombarded daily with readings, friends' opinions, or things going on around me that pull me in two different directions. One minute I will think that we should just keep waiting, and the next minute I will think that we should definitely go ahead with IVF. I don't feel like I have gotten a clear message from You one way or the other, which confuses me too. When I opened my Bible today I felt Your presence, and even though I didn't get an answer to my specific question, I felt peaceful knowing that You met me in the pages of Your Word. It is so amazing to think that Your Spirit knows even Your deepest thoughts. That same Spirit resides in us and guides us every day. How is it that we miss You, Lord? How can I not hear You if Your Spirit lives in me? Is it because I don't want to hear, or because You have closed my ears?

Wednesday, February 23, 2005

(1 KINGS 18:16–39)

ELIJAH BELIEVED IN You with a whole heart, Lord. He made a statement, believing with everything in him, that You would come through. Should I be doing more of that in my life? Should I be making demands on You with belief? I believe that You will move me, Father, and Your Spirit will guide me in making those decisions. I truly believe that You have a plan for us, Lord, but knowing how You want it to come about is the hard part. Do You want us to use medical help, or will You make it happen on its own with Your miraculous power? I ask for Your guidance and direction over the next month.

Friday, February 25, 2005

(1 KINGS 18:16–39)

I CLEARLY SEE PARTS of myself in this story, Father. I am wavering between two opinions daily. I want to believe that You will bless us with a child in Your way, when the time is right, but I also look at our circumstances and feel that using medicine may be the way You choose to work this time. If I place this concern on Your altar, once and for all, will You fulfill Your promise? Will You come down and consume the doubts, angers, disappointments, and hurts and bring our child into being? I want to be as certain as Elijah. Answer me, Lord, so that others will believe. I pray for that with all the faith I can muster.

Wednesday, March 2, 2005

(GALATIANS 4:21–5:1)

SARAH AND HAGAR again—is this my message from You? I have wondered so many times if doing IVF again would mean that we were taking things into our own hands, possibly creating an Ishmael when that's not what You want. A child could come of it, but if it's not Your way, it could cause us heartache in the future (the child of connivance and the child of promise fighting and bringing sadness that isn't necessary). On the other hand, You know what is best, and You can bring goodness and blessing out of everything, but will there be a price to pay for our decision? I really need guidance, because Lee is still really leaning toward doing IVF again. Which way do You want me to go?

Friday, March 4, 2005

I KNOW I HAVE heard You tell me to wait in the past, Lord, but I sensed at the time that You were asking me to wait something out, not wait indefinitely. Now I am at a crossroads, and I don't know how You want me to respond. Many times I have thought that the waiting we have done up to this point has gotten us to a place where I must trust Lee and submit to the decision he feels is right for our family. Is this right? I just can't believe that You would want me to go against my husband when he is not asking me to sin. I have prayed every day that You would speak to his heart and tell him what we should do. Are You speaking to him, and should I follow his lead? At times I think I want that to be true just because I want a child so badly, but when I examine my heart, I know that I want Your will for my life most of all. Help me to discern Your way.

Monday, March 7, 2005

I HAVE BEEN GIVEN such great assurances of Your love today, Father. Lee and I have both felt so weighed down, worried, and lost about Your will for us right now. We feel the date growing closer when we have to call the doctor and let him know whether or not we are going to start the IVF process this month. We have both been searching so hard for signs from You, and we are weary, scared, and tired. We are scared of making the wrong decision and weary of overanalyzing every detail for little glimpses into the plan You have for our future family. Today, as I read my devotion, I was flooded with reminders of Your love that is constant. Fretfulness just gets in the way of truly hearing You, so in our efforts to discern Your will, we have blocked You out. I know I have taken so much responsibility for this decision, like if I choose incorrectly the sky will fall or I will fall out of Your favor or that somehow Your plan won't be fulfilled. How silly I am, how full of myself. You will bring about Your plan no matter what I do and You can bring good out of even the worst choices. I am beginning to think that if Lee and I haven't heard a clear word from You to wait, then moving ahead with IVF will be okay. If You don't want us to have a child yet, then it won't work. You control everything, and our lives are in Your hands. All we can do is honestly seek Your wisdom and guidance and then ask You to bless our decision. I feel so much calmer, less stressed, and more full of Your love. You promised me that I would give birth to children, Father, and I believe that will happen with all my heart. The question now is how and when; questions only You can answer. I wait expectantly...

Wednesday, March 9, 2005

HERE I AM faltering again, thinking I may have heard You wrong, thinking waiting is now the thing to do. Why won't this battle within me come to an end? I really think that since I can't make a decision we should just wait a couple more months. Maybe in that time we will be able to get some more clarity. I am worried about talking to Lee about it tonight because we had already decided that we were going to do IVF, and now I am changing my mind again. Please open Lee's heart to my lament, and help us to move forward together.

Thursday, March 10, 2005

I AM FULL OF "thank you's" today, Father. First of all, thank You for blessing my talk with Lee last night. Before I even finished trying to explain why I thought we should wait on IVF, Lee looked at me, grabbed my hand, and said so gently and sweetly, "Alissa, we can wait, it's okay." I still don't feel a complete sense of peace, just a weight off my shoulders because some kind of decision has been made for a little while. Lee said that waiting a couple months won't hurt anything, and we can keep praying about it for now. He is such a supportive and understanding man—thank You for lending him to me while we are on this earth. I also want to thank You for coming to me again yesterday during the reflection time at the end of my yoga/Pilates class. I saw so clearly a vision of Lee and myself standing together in a huge, open field full of tall grass and wildflowers. We were strolling together, holding hands, talking (although I couldn't hear our words), smiling, and enjoying each other. The sun was shining, and I could feel it on my face. Then we both looked over and saw You coming over the hill in a white, flowing robe, holding something in Your arms. You came right up to us and put a beautiful baby into Lee's arms. We both looked into its eyes with amazement. Then You gathered all of us into Your arms and just held us for a while. I laid my head on Your chest, held Lee's hand, and felt completely full of love. You then walked with us through the field. My vision ended there, but I wonder if this means You are bringing the blessing of a child to us soon. Thank You for all the blessings You have showered upon me in this life so far and for all that are to come.

Tuesday, March 15, 2005

I AM TRYING TO keep the right perspective, living each day fully, as if it were my last. I am trying to lay my worries about the future at Your throne and not think of them again. But there are times when I go crawling back, for some human reason, and let those worries overtake me again. Why do I do this, Father? You have given me a way to live a life free of worry and anxiety, but I hold onto it instead of letting go. Help me truly to offer these things up to You and then move forward to do the work You want me to do, truly unhindered by worry.

Wednesday, March 16, 2005

(NEHEMIAH 6; COLOSSIANS 2:6–3:4)

I WANT THIS RELATIONSHIP with You, this reliance on prayer, this total commitment to Your work and Your purpose for my life. I find myself faltering again only a week after we made the decision to wait for a little while with IVF. I got my period yesterday, so I want to run the other way and call my doctor to get things started right away. I can't base my decision on this one event, though, and on the hormonal feelings that come along with it. I think I had high hopes that, because we decided to wait, we would be pregnant this month, but when that didn't happen, the self-pity started to creep back in. Create a heart and spirit in me, Father, that will not falter but will stand strong when disappointments come. I long for my life to be rooted and built in You at all times and under all circumstances. You have circumcised my heart, Lord, now give me the strength and courage to live like it.

Friday, March 18, 2005

(Jeremiah 6:10, 16–19)

HERE IS ANOTHER example of the Israelites not listening to You, Father. As I read these stories I want to yell and scream at them and tell them just to do what You command and their lives will be so much easier. Yet I am guilty of not listening to You every day, so how can I judge their actions? I know that Your ways are best, but I still continue to choose my ways instead. Why is that? I am starting to feel the battle of this IVF decision beginning again in my mind and heart. Did we make a mistake by waiting? How long should we wait now? Instead of worrying, I should be using that mental capacity to do Your work here on earth. Lord, open my ears to hear You clearly. Open my eyes to see what You lay before me. Open my heart to follow Your commands out of love. Open my mind to know what You know.

Monday, March 21, 2005

(2 Samuel 2)

MY DEVOTIONS AND Scripture reading today made me realize that I need to have a more flexible spirit. I need to bend to Your ways in my life. There will be trials and hardships, but this is Your discipline and correction in my life, Lord. This brings to mind 2 Corinthians 12:9–10, "But he said to me, 'My grace is sufficient for you, for my power is made perfect in weakness.' Therefore I will boast all the more gladly about my weaknesses, so that Christ's power may rest on me. That is why, for Christ's sake, I delight in weaknesses, in insults, in hardships, in persecutions, in difficulties. For when I am weak, then I am strong." If I don't allow You to mold me during these times, I will learn nothing, and I will not bear abundant fruit. Sometimes I think I have Your plan for my life all figured out, only to realize I was wrong and that You have more work to do on me. If I allow the life I am living to be completely guided by You, then I won't have to question whether or not I am in Your will—I will just be there.

Tuesday, March 22, 2005

(John 10:1–5; 14–16)

HERE I AM, Lord, trying to justify the IVF decision all over again. I wish I could say that from the minute I made the decision to wait, I never thought about it again, but that's not the case. I keep wondering if we should still go ahead and do it soon. I know that a part of this uncertainty is because Lee and I aren't on the same page, and I wonder what You are trying to tell me by that. He talks often about why he thinks we should go ahead with it, so it is constantly on my mind. I also think part of it is that my desire for a child is stronger than my desire to hear Your voice. It shouldn't be this way, but I truthfully think it is. Why would You make my desire to be a mother so strong and then deny me a child? I don't understand. As I read John today I realized that I have always found comfort in the analogy of the shepherd and his sheep. A sheep seems so meek and mild, willing to be led wherever the shepherd wants. When I think of a shepherd, I think of a kind and gentle man, who is also strong and commanding so that the sheep will listen to his voice. What I long for is somehow to become that sheep following his shepherd without question. I see myself so often wandering away and becoming stubborn and hurtful instead. But You always come find me and bring me back to Your side. I pray that You give me the heart of a sheep that always recognizes and follows his shepherd's voice.

Thursday, March 24, 2005

(Jeremiah 6:10, 16–19; 1 Samuel 3)

WHY ARE WE, Your people, so stubborn? Why do I tune out Your voice when what I really want is to hear You? As my shepherd, You want to lead me and have me recognize and follow Your voice, but so often I do the exact opposite. At times I will even listen to a stranger's voice rather than yours. Why do I resist? Is it because I know You will ask me to do something difficult? I loved reading 1 Samuel 3, and I so needed to hear those words from You today. I reread verse 20 many times: "The Lord was with Samuel as he grew up, and he let none of his words fall to the ground." It made me wonder how many of Your words I have let fall to the ground. How often have I let my ears be closed to hearing what You had to say to me? It makes me sad to know that I have missed whisperings from You, meant only for me, because of my own hard-heartedness. Father, please help me to catch all Your precious words and listen closely to each one of them so that I won't miss anymore of the wisdom and words of comfort You wish to bestow on me.

Monday, March 28, 2005

WHAT A GLORIOUS Easter day yesterday! I felt Your presence with me all day long. It was rainy and cold outside, but my heart and soul felt alive with thankfulness for the gift of Your Son. I had tears of joy in church as we sang praises, and I felt surrounded by so many blessings. I am right in the middle of my cycle now, so Lee and I set aside some time last night to make our intimate time together special rather than rushed, and it was beautiful. So often during the time of each month when we are trying to conceive, things are forced, but last night wasn't like that at all. We both felt so close to each other, and we prayed right afterward that You would allow us to conceive a child. It all felt so right. Thank You for a beautiful day and for Your amazing gift to the world.

Tuesday, March 29, 2005

I FEEL VERY PEACEFUL before You today, Father. As I sit on my porch admiring Your beautiful creation, I wonder why I allow this peace to leave me so quickly at times. I allow my "to do" list to overwhelm me, instead of tackling each task with joy, expecting to see You in it somehow. I also let my human longing for a child drown out Your words of comfort that everything will happen in Your timing, to bring about the ultimate blessings. I feel so wrapped up in those assurances right now and hope I will be able to say the same tomorrow, tonight, this afternoon, even ten minutes from now. Please help me, Father, to keep You foremost in my mind so Your peace fills me up always.

Wednesday, March 30, 2005

(2 Samuel 7)

DAVID HAD HIS eyes and ears wide open to You, Lord. You answered him with a "no" to building the temple but promised him blessings and long life to his family. He so graciously accepted Your answer and prayed so honestly from his heart. You have given me a promise, Father, which some days I find comfort in and other days I doubt. Give me the strength, patience, and believing heart of David to await the timing of Your plan with joy and anticipation. Help me to accept Your "no" graciously, knowing You have my best interest at heart.

Tuesday, April 5, 2005

(Deuteronomy 6:1–9; Nehemiah 8:1–12)

TRUE OBEDIENCE SEEMS to be the theme in these readings today. We must try to be obedient to all Your commands all the time, and we must be obediently reverent as Your Word is taught and we go forth praising You. This seems to be a monumental task, but if it is done with love, the journey of striving for it can be beautiful. The Deuteronomy passage brings to mind situations in which I could teach my future children about You. I want to be knowledgeable about Your Word so that I can answer them when they have questions. But I must also remember that when I don't know the answer, it is an opportunity to teach them how to pray for Your wisdom and understanding. With children on my mind, I start to wonder where You are leading me right now, Father. What do You have in store for Lee and me in the days to come? I feel my impatience growing each day, and I have to stop and pray for You to remove it from my heart and mind. I am starting to have all the signs of my period, including moodiness, which doesn't help matters. When I made the decision not to do IVF last month, I felt so confident in Your plan. I felt certain that, by waiting, You would bring the miracle of a child into our lives, and then there would be no doubt that it was You. Now, as I prepare for the end to another month of possibilities, I feel less sure, and the thought of doing IVF again starts creeping back into my thoughts often. As I read back over this, I am struck by my use of "I" rather than "we" in the decision making process. Deep in my heart I know that Lee and I must make this decision together, but I don't know how to get there. Please help me to know what to do.

Wednesday, April 6, 2005

FATHER, YOUR WORD says that You "will wipe every tear from their eyes" (Revelation 7:17). What do those tears mean to You? Do You cry with me? Does Your heart ache for me? My love for You is strong and sure, but at times doubts rise up in my mind about Your plan. I wonder if I am hearing You correctly. I even wonder sometimes if Your promise that I will someday give birth to children is all in my head. Did I read too much into it? Where are You leading me? Please enable me to come to You with my doubts, to fall into Your arms when I need to cry, and to listen closely with my head and my heart for Your voice.

Thursday, April 7, 2005

FATHER, I HAVE been so confused about what is from You, what is from my own human mind, and even what may be from Satan as we try to make this decision about IVF. I am hearing voices, but I am at a point where I can't tell which one is yours, my Shepherd. I know that this decision isn't a choice between following Your commands or not, because no where in the Bible does it say, "Thou shall not do IVF," but I want so desperately to do what You want so that Your plan can be fulfilled exactly as You want it to be. You are so much bigger than this decision, and no matter what we choose to do, You can make it work as You want, but somehow I want to be able to move forward with a blessing of sorts. I struggle daily with why You would have Lee wanting something different from what You want. I don't believe that You would make me choose between You and my husband over something that isn't violating Your laws. I feel all this confusion, but Lee seems to be thinking clearly. He has prayed about this so faithfully, and he feels that You have spoken clearly to him through circumstances. Through this entire journey I have prayed for You to reveal, not just to me but to Lee also, what Your will is. Maybe Lee is already there, and I am lagging behind, scared of making the wrong move. Maybe I have to step out in faith, believing that You are leading Lee, and then continue praying that You either bless our decision or change Lee's heart. Maybe this is the boost Lee needs to feel truly like the spiritual leader of our family. Is this the step I have been avoiding? Is this what You want of me? Help me to know, and help me to trust You to lead Lee and me as a family.

Friday, April 8, 2005

(2 SAMUEL 10)

I CAN'T SAY I have any more answers today than I did yesterday, but I do know that You sent me comfort today through my devotion and Your Word. The letter from You in *Come Away My Beloved*[4] said, "I go before You daily to prepare Your way, and You will be accompanied by my goodness and my mercy." I tend to feel as if I have to forge the path, but I should leave that to You and follow Your lead. The second half of verse 12 from 2 Samuel also comforted me today. It says, "The Lord will do what is good in his sight." The *Message*[6] Bible translation of that same verse says, "And God will do whatever he sees needs doing." You can bring about Your will and the blessings You have for us no matter what decision we make. I am feeling more and more like I need to follow Lee's lead. I need to give him the reins as spiritual leader of our family. You brought us together for a reason, Lord. We balance each other so well. Right now I see myself floundering and emotionally scattered, while Lee seems confident and stable in his decision, believing we are in Your will. Help me to know for certain if this is the right thing to do.

Monday, April 11, 2005

MY DEVOTION TODAY was a sweet, gentle reminder of Your presence and Your loving nature toward Your children. I have asked so often for a child, but You have not fulfilled that heart's desire yet. So I will keep on asking, knowing that You hear my longings and want what's best for me. I have come to a peaceful conclusion about IVF. Lord, I have to base my decision on what I see and hear. Lee is so sure that You want us to move forward, so I have told him that I will follow his lead. I have prayed for unity on this, and as he prays he continues to feel we should do it, so I have let go. Now I pray that You will bless this decision or make it very clear to both of us that it is not what we should be doing right now.

Wednesday, April 13, 2005

A SPECIFIC VERSE HAS been repeating itself over and over in my mind today. I guess You want me to glean some morsel of understanding and hope from it. It is 1 Peter 5:6–7, "Humble yourselves, therefore, under God's mighty hand, that he may lift you up in due time. Cast all your anxiety on him because he cares for you." I must hand all my worries over to You and humble myself; then You will lift me up at the perfect time. I continue to pray the same prayer for this decision, and I realize that it parallels these verses. I am giving up control and leaving my worries about it in Your hands. You will make it clear to us if IVF isn't the way You want our child to be conceived. I am filled with a sense of peace, as if a huge weight has been lifted from me, knowing that You are ultimately in control. Father, allow Lee and me to be sensitive to Your plan and pliable in Your hand so that You can form us into the people You want us to be.

Friday, April 15, 2005

(Genesis 15)

I FEEL AS IF I am finally coming out of this fog of confusion that I have been consumed by for months now. I am starting to see that I have allowed the focus to be on me all this time, when it should be on You, Father. I have been working so hard to hear from You but not really listening, or I have somehow turned what I think I've heard into whatever would benefit me. I thought, in my limited human brain, that we must have to wait to do IVF because that is really the only way all this would be a miracle, and it would fit so neatly into my idea of the perfect ending for all our heartache and suffering. I felt so righteous in deciding to wait, but it never really gave me peace, and I could never explain why I thought we should wait. So how could it be from You if I still felt uneasy about it and I couldn't point to a moment or word from You to explain my decision? Various things started to trigger this thought process, and I started to realize that my attitude was all wrong. I was still confused, though, so I handed the decision over to Lee. I was ready to follow his lead because I was so lost, but I still didn't know why. As I read Genesis 15 today, it started to make sense to me. Abraham sandwiched his decision in prayer and then ultimately left the decision up to You by giving Lot the first choice of the land. He believed that You would make the decision for him. I have prayed all these months that Lee and I could be united in our decision, and the fact that we were having different thoughts about it frustrated me. But I kept praying for Your wisdom and discernment for both of us in this decision. Now I believe that I must leave the decision up to Lee because he is the spiritual leader of our family. I don't believe that You would ask me to go against him on this. Now I must pray that You will bless this decision or change Lee's heart if moving forward with IVF is the wrong choice. I had put You in a box, God, thinking there was only one way that You could bring about a miracle. How silly of me to think that I was the righteous one that knew it all. I must hand this over to You, believing that You can bring about Your plan any way You choose. I can feel the worry and anxiety lifting as I write and truly make a decision about this in my heart. I am leaving this in Your hands, Father. Either bless our decision or change the heart and mind of my husband to what You want the decision to be. Give Lee all the wisdom and understanding he needs to make a decision that pleases You and brings our family into Your will.

Monday, April 18, 2005

WITH EACH DAY that goes by, I feel myself believing more and more that I have finally made the right decision. When I thought we should wait, I had the opposite feeling. Each day I felt more unsure of my decision. I think this peace is because I have finally left it in Your hands, and I feel more unified with Lee in our decision together. There are three of us in the midst of this decision rather than just me. I truly believe that You can change Lee's heart if going forward isn't right. I want to have a child so badly, but if Lee came to me and said that he had changed his mind and thought we should wait, I would know and trust that it was from You. Lead us both into a right relationship with You, which will bring about the right choices.

Tuesday, April 19, 2005
(MATTHEW 8:5–13)

I SEE PARALLELS TO our situation right now in this story of the Gentile centurion. My lack of faith becomes more apparent in view of the centurion's humble and true faith. I can't let myself get caught up in the religious aspect of all this. Instead I must focus on following You through my husband right now. I have to trust my prayers to You and Your unfailing love for both of us. I can't allow myself to be sidetracked by anyone else's opinions about what is right or what is the most "Christian" thing to do in this situation. Help me to listen lovingly to others but to hear Your voice the loudest so I will know what You want of me. I pray that other people in our lives will understand that this is an issue between You and Lee and me.

Wednesday, April 20, 2005

FOR THE FIRST time since this decision about IVF started consuming all our thoughts, I am feeling very close to You, like I am right in the palm of Your hand. I feel closer than ever to Lee also. I honestly feel like we are one and united with You. Lee got home late last night from a business trip, and it felt so good to have him back with me. Thank You, Lord, for bringing him safely home. This month I have prayed many times that You would bless our union with a child, ready my womb to carry it, and bring the miracle of life into our lives. Is now the time?

Friday, April 22, 2005

I CAN FEEL YOU in the air today, like an electric current. My day has been filled with confirmations and reassurances, from friends and new acquaintances, of Your love and power. Each day that goes by since I made my decision to let Lee lead us, I have become more confident that I am doing the right thing, and I feel so wrapped up in Your promises of love and protection. Lee and I are closer than ever, and I have a sense of peace that goes beyond the sense of relief over just having the decision made. I continue to pray daily that You will bless this decision or show us the way.

Tuesday, April 26, 2005

FATHER, I MUST ask for Your guidance and wisdom as Lee and I continue to navigate our way through this journey we are on. I found out yesterday that I received some incorrect information concerning our insurance coverage for IVF. They will still cover 80% of the procedure as they did last time, but it won't be 100% as we'd thought. This was one of the ways that Lee thought You were speaking to us, so now I am not sure what he will want to do. Does this mean You don't want us to move forward? We are so blessed to have 80% coverage, and we felt that was a reason to go ahead with it the first time. I ask that You guide us both, and open Lee's heart to know Your will.

Wednesday, April 27, 2005

FATHER, I HAVE been praying for a couple of weeks now that You would change Lee's heart if this IVF decision is wrong. I think that may be happening, which is both exciting and scary at the same time. We went to a program last night, and the theme was adoption. Various people spoke about their experiences with it, and it really made us both think hard about our future. When we got home, Lee said that between seeing that program and the recent change in insurance, he is starting to doubt his original decision. Please be with us and guide us to exactly what You want of us.

Friday, April 29, 2005

I WAS REMINDED AGAIN in my devotion today that the only thing I can and should be certain of is my faith in You and Your love for me. I should embrace uncertainty, because I never know what You are going to put in my path, and I could miss opportunities if I am so concentrated on my routine. I want to wait expectantly to see what Your plan has in store for me, but my impatience often creeps in and changes that expectancy to anger or disappointment. Help me to embrace the uncertainty in my life so that I won't miss any opportunities to praise You and please You.

Monday, May 2, 2005

FATHER, I CAN feel You at work in my life right now and in Lee's life too. Lee still felt uncertain about what to do about IVF when I got my period yesterday. We thought we had a few more days to think about things, so we were surprised when it came early. As we talked about it last night, we both came to the realization that waiting another month wouldn't hurt anything and would give us more time to pray and feel confident about our decision. Lee said that he would like to talk to someone who isn't emotionally attached to this decision and who can give him another Christian, male perspective on it. I felt such peace after we talked, because I feel we are giving ourselves time, and Lee is trying so hard to discern Your will. Once again we are united in our decision, and that just feels so right. So we begin another month of trying to conceive on our own. For some reason I feel especially hopeful that things could work for us this month. I don't know why I feel this way since there doesn't seem to be anything special or different about this month compared to any of the other months in the last four and a half years. Maybe it is because I am having a more normal cycle than I have had in a while. I am pretty sure that I have had another ovarian cyst for the last couple months. I think it is gone now, though, so we may have a fighting chance this month. No matter what, I continue to pray that You will guide Lee as he leads us, and fill me with Your grace to support him along this journey.

Tuesday, May 3, 2005

FATHER, MY DEVOTION today reminded me that I must continuously praise through my trials and struggles. You inhabit the praises of Your people, so if I am continually praising You, Satan has less of a chance to worm his way into my mind. Your Son already won the victory for us, and our main purpose here is to bring more people to You. My wants and desires for a family should not be my focus all the time—spreading Your Word should be. Distraction and discouragement are two things that get me off track so often. Keep me close to You, protected from these things, and focused on You and Your purpose for me here.

Wednesday, May 4, 2005

FILL MY HEART to overflowing with Your Holy Spirit, Lord. Equip me with what I need to do the work You require and desire of me. Allow my wants to scatter to the sidelines as I forge ahead to do what is truly important while I am here on earth. Father, I know there are days when I am full of sadness and discouragement because my wants aren't being satisfied, but I must remember that the victory is won—I have the promise of eternal life with You. This should be enough. Now I must bring others to You to share in that promise. If my heart's desire for a child is granted, it will just be icing on the cake.

Friday, May 6, 2005

I KNOW THAT YOU are working on Lee and me, Lord. I don't know exactly the purpose, but I feel that this journey we are on, this trial You have put in our lives, is for a specific reason. You want to build our strength of character, to teach us how to be confident in You in the midst of hard times. It gets me wondering what is ahead. I, of course, want the future to include a child for us, but if I think too much about that I start to doubt and get sad. Motherhood seems so out of reach. Each day, each month, each year that goes by, it becomes harder and harder for me to imagine what it would be like to have a child to love and nurture. I must have hope and confidence in Your plan, Father.

Wednesday, May 11, 2005

I TOOK SOME MUCH needed time this morning to be silent in Your presence. I know that I don't do this enough, and then I wonder why I can't hear Your voice clearly at times. It seems so simple when I take the time to really think about it. I let the busyness of doing work that is supposedly for You get in the way of true, quality time with You. Just sitting down and reading a devotion every day isn't enough. I need to be silent before You so that You can have a chance to speak to me. Today I just closed my eyes and imagined You and me, face to face. It was so refreshing, and I felt You reassuring me and telling me that whatever Lee and I decide, You will bless. I have an unexplainable sense of peace surrounding me right now. Thank You, Father.

Friday, May 13, 2005

I FIND MYSELF AWAITING Your answer daily, Father. I am trying to be patient, and I am asking You with a pure heart to allow us to conceive a child this month. I don't ever want to look back and realize that I never just asked You to bless us with a child (Luke 11:9–10). I went to my niece's end-of-school program today and felt so out of place. Everyone there had children. There were little babies everywhere, and I stood with empty arms, feeling like an outcast and a fool. I just wish I understood why others are so blessed with families and we aren't. Please continue to give me patience and lessen the yearning in my heart so the sadness will lift.

Monday, May 16, 2005

I WAS REALLY CONVICTED today by the words in *Come Away My Beloved*[4]. I start to feel sorry for myself, wallowing in self-pity, thinking I am so alone in my struggles. But You are always right there, Father. I am just not turning my ear to Your voice or acknowledging Your presence. I ask Your forgiveness for turning a cold shoulder to You and ask You to give me the will to draw near to You once again. Make Your personal presence real to me again, attune my ear to Your voice, and hold me so close to Your heart that its rhythm will guide my steps. Help me not to turn away again to wallow in loneliness and worldly problems. Give me a heart for Your work and guide me in Your ways.

Tuesday, May 17, 2005

FATHER, MY DESIRE to be a mother continues to grow stronger each day, and I continue to struggle with the reasoning of it. Why would You allow this desire to grow in me if You haven't blessed me with a child? Maybe it is so I will continue to have faith in Your promise to me. I find some comfort in the thought that one day Lee and I will have a family, but sometimes, dealing with the sadness and disappointment of the day-to-day waiting overwhelms me. I don't want to become bogged down by all this and lose my strong vision of You delivering a child into our arms, but it is so hard at times to fight off the sadness that wants to swallow me whole. Help me to keep my focus on all the extraordinary blessings of this life—they are everywhere, if I lift up my head and look around me.

Thursday, May 19, 2005

HERE LEE AND I are again, days away from having to make a decision, teetering on the brink of uncertainty. We have been praying about this for weeks, with no clear vision of what You want of us, Father. Lee had a meeting set up with a friend of his to get some solid, Christian advice from someone not emotionally attached to the situation, but it had to be postponed, so we have no other words of wisdom to ponder. We sat down with the calendar and figured out that we either have to do IVF this month or wait until October because of vacations and the doctor's lab being closed in August. To throw another wrench in the works, I just found out that there is an opening for a sold-out conference that I really wanted to go to. However, if we do IVF I would have to turn it down. I could really read the circumstances either way right now, which is very frustrating. What do You want, Lord? I am begging for Your guidance.

Friday, May 20, 2005

FATHER, I AM weary. I am so tired of wondering what our next step should be. Yesterday I talked to a friend who has been through many of the same struggles with infertility. She and her husband have been at a crossroads, too, so it was so helpful to discuss our problems with each other. Something that she said has been replaying itself in my mind ever since we talked. She said that up to this point we have done what we know to do and what You ask of us (praying, submitting to our husbands as spiritual leaders, asking for Your guidance, etc.). Now we must make the best decision we can as humans, and whatever is supposed to happen You will make happen. Those words have given me such comfort. When Lee got home yesterday, he told me that he had gotten a chance to talk to his friend about our situation. As we started sharing our individual stories with each other, it was clear to both of us that, without knowing it, these two friends had given us almost identical advice. Lee's friend gave him a great process he uses to make decisions and also told him that You won't be angry with us if we make the wrong decision. I think we both just needed to hear someone tell us that. He said that at some point we just have to make a decision, or we will drive ourselves crazy trying to read into everything, wondering if it is a sign. His advice was to first lay out all our options, then discuss them and decide which of them are unacceptable. Next, we must make our decision and watch for You to open doors along the way that will lead us in the right direction. You may lead us down a path more wonderful and different than we originally thought possible. We plan on doing a lot of talking, thinking, and praying about it this weekend.

Monday, May 23, 2005

LEE AND I have made the decision to do IVF again. After going through the process Lee's friend recommended, we felt that this was the best decision we could make with what we know. Now we must keep our eyes open for You to guide us down this path, remembering that You will open doors as we go and bring us exactly where we need to be. I feel peaceful knowing that You will bring about the best outcome. I pray that our decisions along the way will glorify You and that we will both speak boldly of Your love and mercy. Guide our steps, Father, and keep our hearts open to Your leading.

Tuesday, May 24, 2005

FATHER, I DON'T exactly understand Your plan, but I am confident that You are guiding us right now. I found out this morning that we are actually going to have to wait until August to do IVF. I called to let the nurse know that we are ready to start, and she said that the lab is going to be closed for two months (June and July), so I will have to wait until August for the procedure. At first I was so frustrated, but then I realized that Your hand was in this and that there is a very good reason that we have to wait. As I prayed this morning, I was reminded that I had said that I wanted really to learn how to embrace the unexpected, which, very likely, is Your working out the circumstances of my life to fit Your plan. I must trust in the fact that You can see my future laid out before You and know what needs to happen. So, thank You, Father, for guiding us and for making Your presence known. I feel You so close to me today and know that this is Your doing. My frustration has been replaced by a feeling of excitement. Somehow I feel as if You are getting things in order and that a wonderful blessing is right around the corner.

Wednesday, May 25, 2005

(1 Kings 17)

I LOVE THIS FIRST story of the prophet Elijah. It shows me so many things that I need to remember in my own life. First, it shows that You will provide, and many times it is in a way we would never imagine. In this case, You used Your power over all creatures to command ravens to bring Elijah food, and they obeyed. Second, the story demonstrates that miracles tend to come after acts of obedience. In the miracle of the flour and the oil, the widow first had to obey, even though she thought it would mean that she and her son would starve. Only then did You allow the miracle to take place. Lastly, You use trials to ultimately bring about Your wonderful plan. The fact that the widow's son was dying seemed to her like a trial she couldn't bear, but again You displayed Your power by saving her son. Through this miracle she came to believe Elijah was truly sent from You. Father, You have provided for Lee and me so abundantly and in ways we never dreamed of. You have met not only our physical needs but also our spiritual and emotional needs. Now we are both trying to be obedient to You and Your will. Maybe a miracle is in store for us too! This trial we are struggling with at times seems so unbearable, and we can't begin to understand why we must walk through it. In the moments when I am focused on You, I know that You will bring something beautiful out of it, something that will glorify You. You are an amazing God, always watching out for Your dear ones.

Thursday, May 26, 2005

I NEED A LARGE dose of patience right now, Father. My body is acting a little strange, and I expected my period yesterday but have had no sign of it yet. I have had light cramps on and off since Tuesday, so I keep thinking it will come any time. Of course, I want to believe that I may be pregnant, but it is really too early to know. It is torturous to wait—each hour that nothing happens I get more excited, even though I tell myself I shouldn't. I need You to fill my mind with other thoughts, leaving the outcome in Your hands. Grant me patience, Lord, and strength for whatever happens.

Friday, May 27, 2005

FATHER, YOU TRULY are the God of miracles. It is hard for me to write this because I can't even believe its true. I am pregnant! You have brought this blessing about in Your time, Lord. There aren't words to describe how grateful and thankful I am that You would bring this blessing into my life right now. Of course, I am also really scared that we will lose this child as we have the others, but I have to try to hand those worries and anxieties over to You, knowing that whatever happens is what is best. It doesn't even seem real, but I know this is a gift from You. Thank You…

Wednesday, June 1, 2005

I AM STILL SOMEWHAT in a daze and can't believe that I finally have a life growing inside of me again. I am really trying to hand over all my anxieties about this pregnancy to You, Father, but at times they still creep in. I want so badly to believe that this is it—that this time everything will turn out all right. This life is truly a gift from You, not something we manipulated—it was just Your perfect timing. I feel my excitement ready to bubble over, but I can't quite let it because I am guarding my heart until we make it through the next ten weeks or so. Please give us both the patience and strength to embrace whatever Your plan has in store.

Thursday, June 2, 2005

I READ TODAY IN my devotion that I must learn to be "haunted by God."[5] My life must be so filled with Your presence that no cares, worries, tribulations, etc., can get in and take over. I needed to hear that right now, because the anxieties and worries of miscarriage are always on the edge of my consciousness, ready to flood in at a weak moment. I am going to try to remember to praise You whenever the doubts and worries come. I will speak, sing, or pray to You so that I am so filled with Your presence that the bad thoughts will be chased away. Help bring this to mind, Father. Invade every corner of my heart and mind so there are no dark corners for the worries to hide and grow.

Friday, June 3, 2005

*H*AVE I LISTENED well enough, Lord? Have I taken the time to hear Your words, Your joys, Your wishes? I think too often I spend all my time with You just worrying about myself and what I am going through, what I need from You. Help me to slow down this summer and get in the habit of just listening to what You have to say. I am sure to find treasures that I never dreamed of. I tend to want to fast forward through the next ten weeks so that I won't worry about every little thing my body does, but instead, I must embrace this time, enjoy the changing of my body as I prepare for motherhood, and enjoy this time alone with Lee.

Tuesday, June 7, 2005

I HAVE A SENSE of peace today that I haven't had since I found out I am pregnant. I have to thank You, Father, for this peace and the things that brought it. I have been so distraught the last few days, allowing the worries and doubts to flood my thoughts. I could barely pray yesterday because my head was spinning, busy thinking of all the "what-ifs." All I could do was ask You over and over again to keep this baby safe and to help me hand this all over to You once again. The time Lee and I spent together last night for our anniversary was so therapeutic. I realized how blessed I am just to have him in my life. He reminded me that we just need to keep looking for the good. The fact that we are pregnant at all is so amazing, and we need to bask in that goodness for however long it lasts. I am going to see my doctor today, which I am sure will calm some of my fears. Thank You again, Father, for this new life that is part of Lee and me. Keep it safe, and help us to enjoy and embrace each moment rather than worrying them away. Remind me often that You only want what is best for the two of us.

Monday, June 13, 2005

ONE STEP AT a time—that is what I must remind myself. All my test results came back, and my hormone levels look good. My progesterone is a little low, so my doctor is having me take a supplement every day. The next big milestone will be our first ultrasound next week. If everything looks good and we see a heartbeat, then we just continue to wait. I love thinking about the fact that there is a little life growing inside me, but there is a touch of anxiety there, too. I know I must banish those thoughts, knowing that You will take care of me. Help me to fill my mind with praises instead.

Wednesday, June 15, 2005

FATHER, YOU TRULY are the God of miracles. I just found out that a friend of mine who has also waited a long time for a child is pregnant. In fact, our due dates are only days apart. How amazing! It makes me think about how all of us are really just here on this earth to fulfill Your plan. We worry, cry, try to take control, but in the end, what You want will always prevail. I don't know that I will ever understand why we had to wait so long, but I can see good that has come from it, and I trust in Your plan.

Thursday, June 16, 2005

HAVE I COMPLETELY relinquished my will to You, Father? I know that is the only way I can truly do Your work, the only way You can work through me. I need to make more of an effort to do this daily—give myself over to You. I fight so hard at times, thinking I am giving up my independence by giving myself over to You, but I know that there are amazing blessings waiting for me if I will truly let go of my life. You have blessed me already so abundantly, and as I wait to finally become a mother, I wonder what more You could possibly have in store for me. You are so mighty and holy and yet You care about every little thing that happens to me. I don't deserve all You have so wondrously given.

Tuesday, June 21, 2005

I AM SO TIRED and sick, Lord, that I am struggling daily just to get basic things done, and my time with You is often cut short. I have a hard time concentrating, because my upset stomach seems to have taken control of my body. I know this is a normal part of pregnancy, and it is well worth it if in the end I can hold my child in my arms. We have our first ultrasound tomorrow, and we are both very nervous. I have no reason to believe that there is anything wrong, but until we see that heartbeat, I know that both of us will be a little nervous. Help us to put our trust in Your plan, Father, knowing You will always take care of us.

Thursday, June 23, 2005

I FELT YOUR PRESENCE with me yesterday, Lord. You were right there to calm me as we waited to do our ultrasound. We were able to see our little one's heartbeat, and so far everything looks good. We will do another ultrasound in two weeks to make sure all is still well. Why is it that I tend to grab the sacrifice of my worries down off Your altar rather than leaving them there for You to shoulder? I found myself so nervous and worked up before my appointment, worrying about all the same things all over again. I prayed all the way there, and You answered by calming my mind and heart.

Thursday, July 7, 2005

FATHER, IT HAS been quite a while since I have written. I have been traveling, and then Josh, Ginny, and Tristan were here for a few days. I have been in Your Word and in prayer, but I just haven't been writing down my thoughts as regularly. We had another ultrasound today, and we were able to see our baby's body with little arm and leg buds growing. What a miracle! The fact that we are pregnant on our own is a miracle, and this new, little life is a miracle. You are such a great God, and many days I feel that I don't deserve all the amazing blessings in my life. Thank You for it all.

Friday, July 8, 2005

FATHER, I AM sitting out on my porch this morning to pray, meditate, and read Your Word. I realize that I feel closer to You when I am surrounded by Your creation, when I can hear the birds singing and the wind blowing through the trees. I want so much for our child to appreciate all of Your wonders and creations. I know that I won't be a perfect mother, but I want to do the best I can with Your help. I want to take every opportunity to teach him or her about Your love and forgiveness. Help me to do this, Lord. Help me to see this child as Yours so that I will concentrate on what You would want him or her to know and learn. Give me wisdom and discernment to do this well.

Tuesday, July 19, 2005

I AM TRULY AMAZED each day that this pregnancy continues. I shouldn't be, since You are in control and made this possible, but I still am. I hit eleven weeks on Saturday. This is farther than we have ever gotten before, and it seems like everything is continuing to be fine. At our appointment this Friday they will listen for the heartbeat with the Doppler. I think both Lee and I will breathe a sigh of relief when we hear that and know we are a day away from being at twelve weeks. I am still feeling very sick, but I have hope that will change very soon. I am really starting to be tempted to tell people, but we have decided to wait until we get back from vacation in Minnesota. I will be just about fourteen weeks then. Thank you, Father, for this little miracle.

Wednesday, July 20, 2005

I AM STRUGGLING, FATHER, with the question of whether or not to do any of this testing to find out if our baby may have Downs Syndrome, spina bifida, etc. My first instinct is not to, because You have already created this child to be exactly who You want him or her to be. Would it really help me any to prepare if I knew ahead of time that there was a problem? That is why the doctors recommend having it done, but I think it might just ruin my pregnancy. There is a good chance for a false positive result also, which I think would just stress me out more. I ask that You move Lee and me in the same direction as we make this decision. Guide us to make the right choice together.

Friday, July 22, 2005

FATHER, I HEARD Your voice clearly this morning. The next step I must take and really start working out in my life is to die to myself daily and to humbly seek a quiet, solitary time with You each day. Not only praying and reading Your Word but also allowing a stronger communication to develop between us. I need to learn not just to sit and do but, more importantly, to sit quietly and listen to Your voice, look into Your eyes, and know You deeply. I have come so far these last eight weeks by learning to turn my anxiety over to You, but now I must move into a new journey with You.

Monday, August 8, 2005

FATHER, ANOTHER MILESTONE of my pregnancy has passed, and all is still well. We heard the heartbeat again on Friday (at fourteen weeks), and it was a beautiful sound. We are both starting to let our guard down a little, and we are beginning to tell our friends the news. I just have to remember that no matter what happens, this is all part of Your ultimate plan for my life. I must rest in the knowledge of Your omniscience and sovereignty in any circumstance that comes. Thank you again, Father, for this miraculous gift.

Conclusion

GOD HAS FULFILLED His incredible promise to me. I now hold my beautiful daughter in my arms and marvel at the miracle God has brought into our lives. He sent our sweet Lucy to us at the perfect time, a time hand-picked by Him long ago. From that tear-filled morning on my front porch when I first heard His promise until now, God has truly led me on a journey down the path of His grace, and continues to with each step I take. At times it seemed so dark, but He has always given me enough light to see my next step. Even with His guidance, there are still many times when I stumble, but again, He is there to lift me up and give me the strength to keep going. He lovingly sprinkles my path with people who bless me with everyday miracles exactly when I need them. And I am sure there are many roadblocks that He removes before I even know they exist.

Prayer has become part of my very existence, and it infuses me with the things I need to make it through each day. I have slowly begun to lift my head up and look deeply into His eyes, rather than constantly looking down at the ground, worrying over each step I take. I know for certain now that the path He has me on is beautiful and perfect—so why take my eyes off His for a moment?

My trust in Him continues to grow stronger, and I have learned to quiet my heart and mind to listen for His voice more often. The child-like faith that I once knew is creeping back into my life, and it gives me such a sense of freedom.

As hard as it may be to understand at times, it is the suffering and trials that bring us closer to God. Along this journey there was pain, disappointment, loss, and fear, but there were more blessings than I can count. We must remember that tomorrow is God's, not ours. So, I pray that you will live in this moment and that through your own, personal trials you will wait with expectation for all the miracles God has planned for your life.

Notes

1. Ann Spangler and Jean E. Syswerda, *Women of the Bible* (Grand Rapids, Michigan: Zondervan, 1999).

2. Linda Dillow, *Calm My Anxious Heart* (Colorado Springs, Colorado: NavPress, 1998).

3. Mary W. Tileston, *Daily Strength for Daily Needs* (London, England: Messrs. Samson, Lowe and Co.,1928), 144. Ella Spees adapted her habits of contentment from a selection by E. B. Pusey (1800–1882) in this book by Tileston.

4. Frances J. Roberts, *Come Away My Beloved* (Uhrichsville, Ohio: Promise Press, 2002).

5. Oswald Chambers, *My Utmost For His Highest* (Grand Rapids, Michigan: Discovery House Publishers, 1992).

6. Eugene H. Peterson, *The Message* (Colorado Springs, Colorado: NavPress, 2002).

www.ingramcontent.com/pod-product-compliance
Lightning Source LLC
Chambersburg PA
CBHW030307080526
44584CB00012B/482